THE FORT WORTH STOCKYARDS NATIONAL HISTORIC DISTRICT

Longhorns, Cattle Brands, Barbed Wire and a Tin Bathtub

~ An illustrated history and guide ~

by
Horace Craig

with special thanks to
Ann Bastable

Library of Congress Card Number: 95-92259

ISBN 1-57502-005-X

Fourth printing (Revised)   July 1999

Additional copies of this book are available by mail.
Send $X.XX each (includes tax and postage) to:
North Forth Worth Historical Society
131 E. Exchange Ave., Suite 110
Fort Worth, TX 76106
(817) 625-5082

Printed in the U.S.A by
Morris Publishing
3212 East Highway 30
Kearney, NE 68847
1-800-650-7888

Thank you for looking at

MORRIS PUBLISHING

Book Specifications

Binding: Perfect binding

Cover: Camera-ready from client
- Printed in full-color
- 10 pt. cover stock & laminated

Text: Typeset by Morris Publishing
- Chapter Heading Style 5
- Text in 11 pt. Times
- Page numbers ~ centered on bottom of pages
- Page headings:
  - Left pages ~ book title
  - Right pages ~ chapter title

Number of Pages: 88 (including this page)

Text Paper: Standard 60 lb. white

Text Ink: Black

Special Pages and Features: Title page, copyright page, dedication page, acknowledgement page, preface, table of contents, pictures and maps, and sources page.

Our commitment to excellence has made us
America's #1 short-run book printer. We are proud
to demonstrate the fine quality of our books.

Dedicated to my dad,
a one-arm Fort Worth policeman

~ George Harris Craig, Sr. ~
1850-1939

Front Cover - Champs - Pen of steers from Burk Burnett's 6666 Ranch brought 12-cents a pound at the 1916 Stock Show. Hog barns, now known as Stockyard Station, are at top right. Photo courtesy of *Star-Telegram* Photograph Collection, Special Collections Division, University of Texas at Arlington Libraries.

Back Cover - Full House - The entertainment at some area-wide events can draw up to 200,000 weekend visitors to the Stockyards. Shown is part of the crowd for Pioneer Days in September 1995.

ACKNOWLEDGEMENTS

Your author is indebted to many Stockyards visitors and others who have suggested the need for an inexpensive publication that would satisfy their hunger to relive the early days of Fort Worth and of the Fort Worth Stockyards. Some have said, "You ought'a write a book!"

Ann Bastable, Manager of the Stockyards Visitors Information Center (Forth Worth Convention and Visitors Bureau) kindly agreed to edit and make suggestions on the rough copy of this effort. I am pleased to have her name associated with it.

Sue McCafferty, who heads the North Fort Worth Historical Society, is the guardian of historic accuracy concerning the Stockyards. Her first-hand knowledge contributed many facts. Her husband, the late Charlie McCafferty, was widely known and admired for his work in preserving this historic legacy.

Ann Kelly, Registrar's Assistant at the Amon Carter Museum, generously read an early draft and made good suggestions. Betsy Hudon, keeper of the *Star-Telegram* photographic collection at the University of Texas at Arlington, was a pleasure to work with as I waded through boxes of photos. The staff in the local history section of the Fort Worth Public Library was a great help, both in research and in photo selection. Mary Jane Ury supplied a photo of the dedicatee, George H. Craig, wearing police badge No. 1. George Smith, retired *Star-Telegram* newsman and editor, pointed out some unstated, understated and misstated facts.

Randy Rothstetter, a genuine cowboy, answered many of my questions about the Texas Longhorn.

My fellow workers at Stockyards Station have also contributed, starting with Allen Short, the boss. Bryan Cherry interviewed me as a tour guide and hired me for my third and most interesting career. Then, I fell in love again — this time with the Stockyards.

Speaking of love, most of all I am indebted to my wife, Loquita. When she didn't want me underfoot, she often suggested: "Why don't you go write a book, or something?"

STATE HISTORICAL MARKERS IN STOCKYARDS

Saunders Park, 100 E. Exchange. Area along Marine Creek walkway honors the Thomas B. Saunders family, prominent in the cattle business. Thomas B. Saunders II was the Stockyards' first cattle dealer.

Fort Worth Stockyards entrance sign. Landmark structure was erected in 1910 and spans the 100 block of E. Exchange.

Thannish Block (Stockyards Hotel), 109 E. Exchange. Marks a fine building put up in 1907.

The Coliseum, 123 E. Exchange. Housed world's first indoor rodeo.

Horse and Mule Barns (Mule Alley), 120 E. Exchange. Was once the world's busiest horse and mule trading center.

Livestock Exchange Building, 131 E. Exchange. Center of one of the great cattle markets of the world.

Fort Worth Stockyards Co., 131 E. Exchange. The yards have been in continuous operation since 1893.

Cattle Brands, 200 E. Exchange. Marker outside the Auction Arena notes that brands have been burned into hides of Texas cattle since 1821.

Hog and Sheep Markets, 140 E. Exchange. Marks a building in which up to a million hogs and two million sheep were traded each year.

Swift & Co., 500 E. Exchange. Over 50 years of meat processing.

Armour & Co., 500 E. Exchange. Over 50 years of meat processing.

Niles City, 2400 Packers Blvd, at E. Exchange. Niles City basically encompassed the Fort Worth Stockyards in its 1.5 square miles and was known from 1911-1923 as the "richest little city in the world."

Mitchell Cemetery, near 28th and Decatur Ave. Contains a dozen graves of pioneers.

Stock Show, outside Billy Bob's Texas. Show began here in 1896.

TABLE OF CONTENTS

THE HISTORY

1. A Cowtown 'Reveille'. 1
2. The Trail Drives 4
3. Crime and Punishment 8
4. The Railroad Comes 12
5. The Big D Connection 16
6. Prosperity Was Named Armour and Swift. 18
7. The End Product 21
8. Some of the Builders 22
9. And Still They Build 27

THE TOUR

10. The Livestock Exchange. 29
11. The Cowtown Coliseum. 32
12. Billy Bob's Texas. 35
13. Horse and Mule Barns. 38

THE WRAP-UP

14. There's Lots to Do in 'Cowtown'. 41
15. Some Milestones. 45
16. The Stockyards Museum. 51
17. Treaty of 1843. 53
18. Cattle Brands. 56
19. The Texas Longhorn. 60
20. Barbed Wire. 62
21. Trail of Fame. 64
22. As the Millennium Ends. 74
Maps 76
Sources 79

PREFACE

Reality for Fort Worth was in the beginning a scratching, clawing, never-say-die hunger for survival. Reality was Hell's Half Acre, a lawless section of downtown Fort Worth that attracted cowboys, railroad workers and buffalo hunters.

Reality was the Indians who were here, the soldiers who came and the settlers who survived. Reality was the heartbreak of many failures and the heart-thumping elation of an occasional success. Happiness was the coming of the railroad and the vestbustin' pride during the short life of the Texas Spring Palace. Reality was the booming prosperity brought by the big Armour and Swift meat packing plants.

Fort Worth from the start has been an oasis for cowboys.

In the 1860s and 1870s, the cowboys came during the trail drive era to rest their herds, to buy their provisions — and to be entertained.

Through the 1880s, the cowboys came to the new railroad to ship their livestock, and stayed to buy their supplies — and to be entertained.

In the 1890s — and for another 50 years after establishment of the Armour and Swift meat packing plants — the cowboys came to market their animals, to buy their hats, boots and saddles — and to be entertained.

Fort Worth and the Stockyards National Historic District today is history that lives. Much still remains to remind what it was. A visit to the Stockyards is a fun-filled, adventurous step into the past that is available nowhere else.

Old-time cattlemen love Fort Worth and the Stockyards. You still see them swaggering in front of the turn-of-the-century buildings and swapping tall tales in the saloons along Exchange Avenue. Old habits are hard to break.

As a stockyards tour guide I was surprised when a young visitor from Germany had her heart set on pushing into a saloon through swinging doors. That's what she wanted the West to be. We no longer have saloons with swinging doors. Even cowboys have come to appreciate air conditioning, and swinging doors aren't efficient. So saloons have changed. The West has changed also...and yet it hasn't.

This book is about 150 years of change, and of much that hasn't changed.

The best way to get a feel for what it was is to explore what is left.

To know the Stockyards, you first must know Fort Worth. That is where this guide begins.

The rest is a story of the evolution of a quiet piece of prairie three miles north of town into one of the world's busiest livestock markets.

Enjoy your trip to the Fort Worth Stockyards. There will never be another place like it.

1

A Cowtown 'Reveille'

You stand in the Fort Worth Stockyards at the world's finest reminder of the adventure, the romance, the enterprise and the tenacity of those who settled the West.

Had you stood here 150 years ago, you would have been afloat in a sea of grass — a gently rolling prairie was broken here and there by generous ribbons of cross timber. All was drained by the Trinity River and its tributaries. There was food and water aplenty for the deer that lived here, and for the buffalo that mig

The land was inhabited by Ind   ren't very hospitable to the few settlers coming thi   es roamed to the north and west, Apaches and Li   est and south. There also were Kiowas, Wacos, Delaw   Tonkawas.

So it was in 1849, when Major Ripley Arnold and a troop of soldiers were ordered to North Texas to protect the scattered settlers along the frontier. The pony soldiers rode upon a bluff above the confluence of the West and Clear Forks of the Trinity River and gazed out over the rich panorama.

One soldier opined it was the most beautiful spot he had ever seen: "Buffalo all around. There were more panthers than I have seen before or since. Antelope without number, and wild turkeys in every tree."

The soldiers built a camp here and it was soon designated a fort.

By now the town already had acquired its fondest description: "Where the West Begins." The phrase resulted after Indians by treaty agreed to remain west of a line that ran through Fort Worth.

The soldiers remained at Fort Worth for only four years. By 1853 the frontier had moved 100 miles to the west and Fort Worth's troops moved to a new line of outposts.

Buildings abandoned by the soldiers became an instant town. One merchant set up shop in a barracks. A competitor took over one of the officer's quarters. The dirt-floored cavalry stable became Fort Worth's first hotel. Another crude building was the school.

After the soldiers left, B. B. Paddock, editor of *The Fort Worth Democrat*, recalled "There was nothing permanent to arouse enthusiasm...no cattle trails, no current of trade, only a few meager settlers."

It was a town that should have died, but didn't.

The credit goes to the optimists who fought not only for survival of the town, but who dared dream of prosperity. If the town was to survive and prosper, its ambitious leaders decided, Fort Worth must somehow acquire the county seat from nearby Birdville.

The issue came to a vote in 1856, and the good citizens of Fort Worth set out to steal the election. First, "someone" made off with a cache of liquor with which Birdville had planned to "attract voters." Then Fort Worth recruited residents from nearby counties to vote illegally. As the crowning blow, cowboys from Fort Worth drove a wagon to the Birdville courthouse, loaded the county records and raced back to Fort Worth. By the time the alarm was sounded in Birdville, it was too late.

Fort Worth "won" the disputed election by just 13 votes and has been the county seat ever since. The incident caused hard feelings for years and resulted in at least two fatal gunfights.

Being a county seat didn't assure survival. During one of its many economic slumps, the town became known as "Panther City." A Dallas newspaper reported business so slow in Fort Worth that a live panther was spotted sleeping undisturbed on Main Street. It was a story that very well could have been true, but Fort Worth ignored the intended slam and adopted the panther as its mascot!

Civil War brought more hard times. There was little to buy and nothing to buy with. Residents carted cotton by hand and laboriously wove it into cloth on a hand loom. Children went barefoot year 'round for lack of shoes.

Wagoneer John White helped supply the town's basic needs. He periodically loaded his wagon with hides, pecans and other produce, hitched up his six-yoke oxen team and plodded toward Houston on a poorly-marked trail. Six weeks later he arrived back in Fort Worth with sugar, coffee, whiskey and other yearned-for goods. White's arrival always was reason for celebration.

The area's greatest need was more settlers. Attracting them was a never-ending challenge. Optimistic developers described Fort Worth as the "Queen City of the Prairie," a veritable Eden of opportunity.

Under a headline that demanded, "Stop that wagon!" the *Democrat* pointed out: "He has been six weeks on the road. He has some money, from two to four horses, a good wagon, and his boys are large enough to do general farm work."

So sell him some land and keep the family here, was the advice.

The small herds that moved through town even before the Civil War earned the town a nickname that to this day suits it best — "Cowtown."

Fort Worth's first love and its enduring marriage has been with livestock and with those who work livestock. The city still is "Cowtown" in heart, body and soul.

With the Civil War over, Fort Worth found itself at the front edge of the colorful trail drive era. A growing tide of longhorn cattle was about to wash through the city and change it forever.

2

The Trail Drives

If the early 1870s found panthers asleep in the streets, the cats certainly scat out of the way for the growing number of trail herds that plodded through downtown Fort Worth during the rest of the decade.

The herds brought with them a spurt of prosperity as eager cowboys bought what entertainment and luxury they could afford.

By the end of the decade there were 37 saloons, 17 blacksmith shops, 24 wagon yards, six hide dealers and seven barbers in town.

Hutton & Peter Bathhouse in November 1873 advertised: "One hundred dozen clean towels always o

How did this prosperity co dit the cattle drives.

After the Civil War th nger through the land, a desire to put meat on the table huge demand arose for beef. At the same time the open ranges Texas were overrun with wild longhorn cattle.

All a fellow had to do was round 'em up, put his brand on 'em, and they were his. They weren't worth much in Texas, maybe $2 a head. But if a cowboy could deliver them up north, they might bring as much as $40 a head. This incentive ignited a 20 year trail drive era.

The object of the trail drives was to deliver Texas cattle to the nearest railroad which, in 1866, was in Kansas. Fort Worth was smack dab in the middle of what has come to be known as the Chisholm Trail.

The herds came from as far away as the Texas coast below San Antonio, trailed roughly the present-day route of I-35, moved through downtown Fort Worth on Rusk (now Commerce Street), and alongside what is now the Fort Worth Stockyards. The trail crossed Indian Territory in Oklahoma and finally terminated at Abilene, Kansas.

The longhorns originally came from Spain and are believed to have been introduced to the new world on the second voyage of Christopher Columbus. The hardy animals came north from Mexico and multiplied as they grazed the open lands of Texas.

Many a Texas rancher got his start by rounding up wild longhorns and grazing his new herd on public lands. The cattleman thereby acquired an instant ranch with a very small investment.

Earning profit off the cattle was another matter. Getting the animals to market involved a drive of hundreds of miles. A trail boss must be selected, a dozen cowboys hired, a cook taken on, and a wrangler selected to handle the 60 to 100 horses in the remuda.

The remuda should contain half a dozen horses for each cowboy. Many of the mounts would be "specialists" — some good in brush, some good for roping, some for night riding, some for cutting.

Many horses remained spirited even after being broken. The first item of business for a cowboy each day was to gain control of his pitching horse. This provided a bit of rodeo excitement each morning as cowboys prepared for the day's drive.

The trail drives were important to Fort Worth so the newspaper carried a regular "box score" each season.

"Fifty-six droves of cattle have passed through Fort Worth this spring," the *Fort Worth Democrat* reported on May 3, 1873. "The largest drove numbered 6,000, the smallest 550. The aggregate of the 56 droves is 62,235. The average drove numbered 1,111."

The peak year for the drives through Fort Worth was 1871, when more than 600,000 animals went up the trail from Texas.

Will Crittendon was one of the estimated 5,000 black cowboys who worked the Chisholm Trail. He was only 9 in 1877 when he helped take his first herd through Fort Worth. Crittendon's charges plodded through the downtown section, then snaked down the bluff to cross the Trinity River.

The river was on a fall rise, Crittendon later recalled. It was the first time the youngster had ever crossed a river on a horse. A horse swells to help it swim, but Crittendon had forgotten to loosen the saddle straps. His horse couldn't swell. Young Crittendon almost lost the animal before getting it back to the bank.

Cowboys arriving at Fort Worth with their herds still faced a 400-mile drive. Cows plod along at 10 to 15 miles a day. Under the best of conditions the cowboys could expect to be on the trail for another 25 days. If they came to a flooded river, met unfriendly Indians or experienced a stampede (which happened often with the wild longhorns), the cowboys could be on the trail for another three months. There was little civilization this side of Kansas.

So Fort Worth with its wild and lawless "Hell's Half Acre," appealed to the young, eager-for-excitement cowboys. Drovers rested and watered their herds around Fort Worth, and the cowboys rode into town prepared to blow a whole month's pay on a bath, a haircut, a warm meal, and a fling in the saloons, gambling houses, dance halls and bordellos.

Along with the drovers from the cattle drives, an estimated 1,500 buffalo hunters operated in West Texas during the 1870s. Fort Worth became a major shipping point for buffalo hides, and "Hell's Half Acre" had yet another group to entertain. The buffalo hunters came to town to sell their hides for $1 each, and to whoop it up in "The Acre."

In the 1870s you could rent a bed in Fort Worth for two-bits or buy a cold shower for a quarter. And heaven only knows how refreshing a good scrub could be after weeks on the prairie.

Offensive odor seemed a way of life.

A 10-feet-high mound of buffalo hides piled in the sun alongside the railroad track added to the city's unique aroma. Buffalo hunters always were easy to identify. Even soap and water wouldn't rid these frontiersmen of their stench.

To make matters worse, city fathers yielded to pressure to repeal a "hog ordinance." The newspaper complained that "The swine may again grunt complacently on our streets."

Unsanitary conditions of the alleys and backyards of the town assaulted the nose. "No place can be healthy and tolerate the odious and offensive odors that arise," commented the newspaper. The article mentioned piles of refuse on South Side properties. "The breeze from that quarter wafts the sickening odors all over Fort Worth," the article commented.

A Fort Worth visitor at the time was wildly entertained when fire broke out. A pistol shot sounded the alarm. Other shots rang out as volunteers acknowledged the emergency. A boy who lived across from the M. T. Johnson Hook & Ladder Co. dashed to the station and clanged the fire bell until volunteers arrived to tow the fire apparatus.

Theater Comique sponsored daily parades to lure customers. An aerialist regularly walked a wire stretched across Main Street in front of the saloon. No doubt a barker outside hinted at the wonders to be enjoyed inside.

Saloons ranged from a crude shack with dirt floor to the more ornate. The First and Last Chance Saloon on the southwest side of the square was a small, dingy room operated by Ed Terrell. There were a few shelves on the west wall on which sat a few bottles of spirits. The bar was a plain, varnished wooden counter. A bucket of drinking water with dipper sat on the bar. Jess Ferguson played a fiddle and revelers sat on a bench along the east wall.

Train robber Sam Bass, who was known to visit Fort Worth, sometimes worked as a trail driver. On one occasion he started up the trail with a herd of 2,000 steers that he had legally purchased. His herd miraculously had grown to 4,000 by the time it reached Abilene, Kansas. Was it luck, or was it a bit of creative rustling en route?

Fort Worth newspaper editor Paddock called Abilene "The wickedest and most God-forsaken place on the continent."

After cowboys disposed of their trail herds there, said Paddock, "They turned their steps to the flaunting dens that offered iniquity in every conceivable form."

He could have been describing Fort Worth's own Hell's Half Acre.

c h a p t e r

3

Crime and Punishment

Rampant sin bothered some of the good folks of Fort Worth, but not enough that they would suffer the economic impact of shutting down "Hell's Half Acre."

In fact the newspaper — either in agony or with braggado — once noted that, due to the town's growth, Hell's Half Acre "now requires two and a half acres."

The area was an island of sin in the center of Fort Worth. Here were many of the saloons, the shooting galleries, gambling and dance halls and bordellos sought out by the bored cowboys.

To the lonely cowhand the Acre was a welcome break from the monotony of the trail. On the other hand, the good folks of Fort Worth saw it as a detriment to decent family life. It was perplexing.

There were many attempts to control, regulate or even outlaw the district. The City Council at one time prohibited dance halls and closed the gambling houses. Businessmen quickly complained that enforcement of the law was too strict. There was nothing to attract cowboys to town. The bored cowpokes simply stayed with their herds outside town. Practical economics came into play and the ordinances were repealed.

The council devoted its time to other matters and Hell's Half Acre survived even beyond the trail drive era.

The council once voted a $5 fine be levied against any cowboy who illegally tied his horse to the new Courthouse fence. To increase revenue, it taxed prostitutes a part of their fines, but reduced the fine for drunkenness from $3 to $1 — a more affordable amount.

As a measure of prosperity, the newspaper once noted that arrests were running about 43 per day — most for drunkenness. "This has led to the belief that the saloons are being more heavily patronized than before," the writer calculated.

Most of the earliest crime was simple drunkenness. No one had much of anything worth stealing.

The city had its first jail by 1868. It was a shed from which escapes were commonplace. One man stayed in the windowless hut as long as he could stand it. He broke out and went to find the marshal, telling the lawman he wasn't about to return to such a disgraceful jail. And he didn't.

Most lawbreakers were as crude as gullibility allowed. In January 1887 residents were warned that counterfeit twenty dollar bills were being circulated.

"The paper is heavier than the real thing and feels greasy to the touch," the newspaper advised. "The word 'taxes' on the back is misspelled 'tares,' and 'engraved' is spelled 'engroved.' The note also is shorter than the genuine article."

Anyone have change for a Twenty?

Newspapers complained of all manner of criminal activity — from the serious to mere irritations.

Some crimes must have seemed worse than others. The *Democrat* bravely noted that "The high hats at the opera must go! They are a nuisance." Or an even worse sin:

"A man has a right to walk on both sides of the sidewalk, but not at the same time."

Some things you just don't tolerate.

Fort Worth had more than its share of stage and train robberies. A favorite point for jumping a stage was at the Mary's Creek Crossing just west of the city. It was believed the culprits eluded the law in Hell's Half Acre. Few were ever caught.

Butch Cassidy and the Sundance Kid also avoided the Fort Worth jail. They and their Hole-in-the-Wall Gang fled to Fort Worth after robbing a bank in Nevada in 1900. They walked the streets of Fort Worth undetected. Law officers figured them to be in hiding "up north."

The Kid's vanity finally did them in. He persuaded the gang to pose for a portrait in a downtown Fort Worth studio. The photographer liked the photo and placed it in his front window for advertising. Did some window shopper recognize the gang? Possibly, for Butch and Sundance quickly left town. The gang broke up and never again operated as a unit.

9

Ironically, the infamous Hole-in-the-Wall Gang members behaved themselves while in Fort Worth. The city's most noted gunfight occurred 15 years earlier and involved two local citizens.

On a cold February night in 1887, Luke Short, owner of the White Elephant Saloon and a noted gambler, was called outside by a former city marshal, the popular "Longhair" Jim Courtwright. The saloon then was in the 300 block of Main St., just north of Hell's Half Acre.

Minutes later, pistols were drawn.

Courtwright had a reputation as an excellent gunman and was fond of saying, "Maybe God can make one man superior to another in physical strength, but when Colt made his pistol, he made all men equal."

But on this night, Courtwright was outdrawn. He was hit by three shots and killed.

Stunned citizens of Fort Worth took up a collection and gave Courtwright the grandest funeral the town had ever seen. They held Short blameless, because it was a fair fight.

One version of the face-off between former friends was that Courtwright was selling protection to businesses in "The Acre" and was attempting to force his extortion on the White Elephant. Short would have none of it. Whatever the real cause, the dispute escalated until neither man felt he could back down.

As city marshal in the 1870s, Courtwright was a master at walking the fence. He kept the respectable folk happy by selectively enforcing the law, and he gained the admiration of those in "the Acre" by looking the other way when he could.

He was held in such esteem that his friends here once helped him escape custody after he was arrested on a New Mexico murder charge. Under heavy guard, Courtwright was brought into a cafe for breakfast. He dropped his napkin and asked a deputy to pick it up for him. "Pick it up yourself," he was told. When Courtwright straightened up he was holding a pair of pistols that had been hidden under the table by friends. Courtwright escaped. He later surrendered and was acquitted of the murder charges.

Luke Short was in another scrape after killing Jim Courtwright. On Christmas Eve in 1890, Short tangled with fellow gamblers at the Bank Saloon and Short suffered a small wound to the hip and to several fingers of the left hand. He claimed the affray was over a crooked game being run at the saloon. A crooked game, he said, was an affront to all honest gamblers. Short died of natural causes in the 1890s and is buried in Oakwood Cemetery, a stone's throw from Courtwright, the man he outdrew that night in 1887.

Butch Cassidy - The Hole-in-the-Wall Gang met its downfall when it posed for this photo in Fort Worth in December 1900. Sitting left to right are Harry Longabaugh (Sundance Kid), Ben Kilpatrick, and George Parker (Butch Cassidy). Standing are Will Carver, left, and Harvey Logan (Kid Curry). Photo courtesy of Amon Carter Museum.

chapter

4

The Railroad Comes

The cowboys and buffalo hunters in Hell's Half Acre were about to welcome a new group of pleasure seekers — the equally thirsty railroad workers.

Fort Worth was about to get its first "iron horse" and, with it, undreamed-of prosperity.

Getting the first railroad to Fort Worth was a jerky trip of emotions coming in waves of elation and despair.

The first wave of hope for a railroad started in 1872. Rumors spread that the Texas & Pacific would push its line westward to Fort Worth. John Weiss Forney, a Philadelphia journalist traveling with a party of potential investors, wrote a glowing account of Fort Worth, concluding: "The view out from this plateau is grand beyond description."

Fort Worth spirits soared, even as railroad builders demanded 320 acres for railroad yards. The land was donated immediately by K. M. Van Zandt, E. B. Daggett, Thomas Jennings and H. G. Hendricks. The town's population soared to 4,000 as a surge of new residents arrived on a tide of high expectations.

Paddock, editor of *The Fort Worth Democrat*, confidently ran a map inside the paper showing a network of railroads that soon would reach Fort Worth from all directions. One scoffer looked at the map and said, in effect, "Why, that looks like a dern tarantula!" The map became known as the "Tarantula Map."

Spirits sagged with the national panic of 1873 caused by the failure of the financial house of Jay Cooke & Co. Work on the railroad was halted. The track work was abandoned at Eagle Ford east of Dallas — more than 30 miles short of Fort Worth.

12

Fort Worth stores closed as rapidly as they had opened. Fort Worth lost three fourths of its population as 3,000 of its 4,000 residents gave up and left town.

"Grass literally grew in the streets," wrote Paddock. "This was not a metaphor to indicate stagnation but a doleful fact."

By 1875, Fort Worth leaders despaired of the road ever being completed by out-of-state investors and undertook to build it themselves. Fort Worth organized a construction company, subscribed the necessary capital from local sources, then entered into a contract with the railroad for completion of the line to Fort Worth.

Not long after this, the enthusiasm of railroad officials was renewed by an offer from the state Legislature of 20 sections of public lands for every mile of track laid. Railroad officials now added their weight to the construction project.

Still, the prospects for success were grim because of a deadline imposed by the state. The land grant offer was only good if the railroad reached Fort Worth by the adjournment of the Legislature in 1876.

The Legislature, having finished its business in July, was ready to adjourn. Tarrant County representative Nicholas H. Darnell was seriously ill, but to gain time, he had friends carry him into the House chambers each morning for 15 days so that he could vote against adjournment. The extra two weeks were enough to allow Fort Worth's citizen-army of railroad builders to complete the line.

Determined Fort Worth residents left their jobs or closed their businesses and literally went out to work alongside the railroad hands in laying track. Saloons sent out free refreshments and womenfolk prepared food.

The track reached Sycamore Creek. There was no trestle and no time to build one. Railroad ties simply were stacked into the creek and the rails were spiked to the make-shift bridge. It would have to do until a proper trestle could be built.

From the creek, the track left the right-of-way and "took to a dirt road." Ties were laid on the rutted lane supported by rocks at each end, and rails were spiked to the ties.

The tracks were "crooked as the proverbial ram's horn," Paddock, later recalled. But it worked! The first train wobbled into town at 11:23 a.m. on July 19, 1876 to a great, spontaneous celebration.

The *Democrat* cautioned: "Our police officers should exercise discretion and lenience to the railroad hands, to be paid off here. They have worked hard and will have their fun."

Most of the railroad hands were paid off in the afternoon. "Drunken men were as thick as fleas on a white dog's back," the *Democrat* later observed.

The railroad proved to be the mother lode that Fort Worth citizens had hoped it would be.

"Instead of having freight brought in with ox and mule team, it will be whirled in at the rate of 15 miles an hour," the newspaper boasted.

For a time the city was "the end of the line." Stage routes to all points not served by the railroad now radiated from Fort Worth. New residents and businesses moved in; buildings and houses sprang up everywhere. Hundreds of new arrivals lived in tents.

The first load of freight out of Fort Worth was flour from the city mill. By 1882, Fort Worth was shipping 350,000 head of livestock per year. This time the prosperity was real.

The first railroad attracted others. The Santa Fe Railroad arrived in 1881 and the Fort Worth & Denver Railroad the next year. Even more lines followed. Paddock's 1873 "Tarantula Map" proved prophetic. Fort Worth had become a major rail center.

The popular editor boasted of the T&P's arrival, passengers "no longer will be subjected to the fatiguing trial of a day's ride in the lumbering coach from Dallas, but can ride comfortably and enjoyably in a little more than an hour."

Anticipating the coming boom, one alderman suggested that Fort Worth might even annex its rival city Dallas!

Dallas?

Now that's a horse of a different color!

Fire Wagon - By 1907 Fort Worth had a three-bay central fire station with a motorized truck serving alongside two horse-drawn wagons. Photo courtesy of Fort Worth Public Library.

That's Entertainment - Just about everyone in town watched as firemen fought a hopeless battle to save the Texas & Pacific Depot in 1904. At left is a monument honoring Al Hayne, hero of an 1890 fire at this spot which destroyed the Texas Spring Palace. The marker still stands at Main and Lancaster. Photo courtesy of Fort Worth Public Library.

15

5

The Big D Connection

Fort Worth and Dallas — about the same age and both hungering for growth — are separated by only 32 miles. It isn't surprising that a wagonload of competitiveness has fermented a lively feud between the two cities.

The success of both Dallas and Fort Worth is an aberration. Neither city should have survived and prospered as it has. There is no great stock of raw material to fuel manufacturing and no navigable waterway to accommodate trade. But survive they h

A journalist once said the two ___ ___ e two hogs at a feed trough: They fight a lot, but the ___ ___ in the process.

The fight continues ___ ___ both cities bickering over a variety of subjects. It is ___ ___ g to go back a dozen decades to the early sparring matches.

In 1873, *The Fort Worth Democrat* chided its neighbor to the east over its crime. "No one has been killed in Dallas since day before yesterday, that we know of."

After the coming of the railroad to Fort Worth, *The Dallas Herald* advised its readers: "For a perfectly boring excursion, take the train to Fort Worth."

The Fort Worth Democrat countered: "Fort Worth's first acquisition from the extended railway will be the bummers and deadbeats and roughs and whiskey guzzlers of Dallas...those unhanged will die of whiskey."

During the panic of 1873, when Fort Worth's business was at a standstill, the *Dallas Herald* stated that a visitor to Fort Worth had seen a panther asleep on Main Street, "unmolested and undisturbed."

Rather than taking exception to the story, Fort Worth adopted a panther as its fire department mascot, and the *Democrat* included an engraving of a panther in its masthead. The baseball team became the "Fort Worth Cats."

Part of the celebration when the railroad arrived was a banquet consisting of panther steaks, panther stew, panther roast and panther-tail soup.

A panther still adorns Forth Worth police badges.

In an obvious slam at its handy opponent, the *Fort Worth Democrat* noted that a Dallas resident had scooped up a bushel of sand from a Dallas street and carried it to his backyard. The paper added, "By the time the fleas jumped out only a quart of sand was left." Such was the humor of the day.

Amon Carter, longtime publisher of *The Fort Worth Star-Telegram*, is said to have always taken his lunch when he visited Dallas because he didn't want to buy anything there.

In 1936, when Dallas was selected as the official site of the Texas Centennial celebration, Fort Worth hired Billy Rose — at a handsome fee during this Depression year — to build and stage Fort Worth's competing Frontier Celebration, including the ambitious Casa Manana Theater. Fort Worth interests leased a billboard across from the entrance to the Dallas Fairgrounds advising showgoers, "Visit Dallas for culture. Visit Fort Worth for fun!"

Sometimes the competitiveness reaches the absurd. The Dallas-Fort Worth Turnpike was built in 1953 to provide a convenient link between the two cities. Even this so-called cooperative venture generated paranoia. Great care was taken to insure that the groundbreaking ceremony was staged exactly mid-way between the two cities.

The squabbling back and forth across the Trinity continues to this day, with most of today's dispute over who gets the advantage in most traffic at the international and regional airports. It is said that the United States and England are two countries separated by a common language. Dallas and Fort Worth are two cities separated by a common airport.

Yet, the Dallas-Fort Worth Airport, one of the biggest and busiest in the world, pumps lifeblood into both modern cities. But risk denial from both if you suggest that either city has anything in common.

Since Fort Worth is known as the city "Where the West begins," it didn't take some wag long to counter, "Yeah, and Dallas is where the East peters out!

chapter

6

Prosperity Was Named Armour and Swift

The beginning of the Twentieth Century marked a decade of amazing growth for the city. If the coming of the railroad was a shot in the arm for Fort Worth, the arrival of the Armour and Swift meat packing houses was a heart transplant. Fort Worth again found booming prosperity.

As early as 1876 *The Fort Worth Democrat* envisioned a meat packing enterprise for Fort Worth. "Steaks should be sweet and juicy," the newspaper noted. "Yet, cattle arrive in North exhausted from riding in a crowded boxcar with little er. They suffer shrinkage. The juices in their meat d. And those Northerners must eat dry, tasteless st

To persuade cattlem need for packing houses, the paper reasoned: "The establishment of refrigerators (meat packers) near the great breeding fields will create a home market, and enable producers to get a better price."

Fort Worth had its railroad (more trunk lines had quickly followed the first), and the city enjoyed a strategic location. It was estimated there were one million head of cattle within 100 miles of Fort Worth.

The city's first attempt at meat packing came in 1881, when an entrepreneur was given six acres on which to build a plant. Unfortunately, the plant was designed exclusively for the slaughter of hogs — and hogs were not what Texas was about. The plant soon closed.

In 1883, Fort Worth leaders subscribed $60,000 to persuade Continental Beef Co. to build a plant on 27 acres. It began operations in February 1884, but Continental attempted to market its carcasses in

St. Louis which, one observer said, was "like sending coal to Newcastle." The firm was bankrupt by year's end.

Isaac Dahlman formed Dahlman Dressed Beef Co. in November 1890 and had in hand a contract to deliver 200 head of dressed beef per day to Liverpool, England, via Galveston. The meat arrived in poor condition, and Dahlman's company went the way of the first two efforts.

Earlier, in 1887, local businessmen raised $30,000 and incorporated the Union Stockyards — on the same site as today's Fort Worth Stockyards. The yards were located on 258 acres with an initial capacity of 5,000 cattle, 10,000 hogs and 1,500 horses and mules. The cattle pens later were enlarged to hold up to 13,000 head of cattle.

Local businessmen also pledged $500,000 capital and organized Fort Worth Packing Co., which opened in November 1890. In its first month it processed 8,340 hogs. It was apparent, however, that a major meat processor was needed if Fort Worth was to become a successful meat packing center.

It was in 1892 when Boston financier Greenlief Simpson and party were persuaded to inspect the Fort Worth Stockyards. They saw pens crammed full of animals — a veritable sea of horns. No doubt they were impressed. Of course, no one in Fort Worth bothered to tell them that flood waters had destroyed a bridge. What they were looking at was a seven-day backup of cattle!

Simpson was the catalyst that got major meat packers interested. The Chicago packers, Armour & Co. and Swift & Co., came to realize that one-fifth of all the cattle in the United States were located in Texas, New Mexico and Oklahoma. It cost up to $5 per head to transport cows to the existing packers. To locate near the source made economic sense.

Armour and Swift demanded and received $50,000 each toward the building of their new Fort Worth plants. Construction on the massive slaughter houses began March 13, 1902. Fort Worth now became one of the world's major livestock markets — and remained so for years.

By 1908, Armour and Swift each had doubled the original capacity of their plants. To entice railroads to extend their lines into the Stockyards, each railroad was offered the necessary right of way for only $1. Trail herds that once walked through town by the thousands now arrived mostly by train and numbered in the hundreds of thousands.

On a normal day, a 1930s era Swift & Co. publication noted, its 1,500 employees would process about 5,000 animals. Placed end to end, a day's requirement would form a line of animals seven miles long.

Plant workers were fast and efficient. Hog carcasses were in the cooler 20 minutes after the animals entered the building. Beef passed "from pen to cooler" in only 35 minutes.

Meantime, the huge central yard was a panorama of sound and motion as trades of up to 5,000,000 head a year were made. Seven switch engines were kept busy shuttling the railroad boxcars to the busy Stockyards sidings.

The meat packers prospered until livestock marketing underwent revolutionary decentralization in the late 1950s. Livestock now moved by truck and competing packers could build anywhere. Meat packers no longer had to be near a railroad to receive cattle.

Local auctions and commercial feedlots also helped change the marketing of cattle. Fort Worth's massive meat packing plants, now over 50 years old, suddenly had to compete with smaller, more efficient meat packers. The end was near.

Armour & Co. closed its Fort Worth plant in 1962. The Swift plant lasted another nine years.

The loss of the meat packing plants which had employed as many as 5,000 workers was devastating to the city. Ironically, during the early 1970s few were interested in investing in the Stockyards. Therefore, for years little was disturbed in the area.

The Fort Worth Stockyards National Historic District came into being in 1976.

The result is something akin to opening the tomb of an ancient king. Much of the Fort Worth Stockyard remains intact.

The discovery provides a continuing historic adventure for those who today "discover" the Fort Worth Stockyards.

7

The End Product

A question often asked as visitors ponder the vastness of the stockyards and the size of the daily kill at Armour and Swift is "What did they do with all the waste?"

The happy answer is that meatpackers utilized as much of an animal as possible. This increased the worth of an animal "on the hoof." Cattle raisers arguably benefited from better prices, the packer through higher profits, and the consumer through lower cost of the end product.

Besides the harvest of edible food, li~~~~ also yielded hides for leather along with numerous other ~~~~ Also used were hair, fat, blood, internal organs an~~~~ ~~~~ings, bones, hooves and horns.

These processing by~~~~s became everything from soap to violin strings.

Meat processing by-products went into shoes, belts, purses, glue, lubricating oil, lard, oleomargarine, synthetic rubber, fertilizer, canned dog food, insecticides, disinfectants, glycerol for explosives, combs, buttons, tennis racket strings, paint brushes and surgical stitches, among others.

Brains, sweetbreads, tongues and oxtails became gourmet foods.

Medicinal innovations helped in treatment of anemia and asthma and other maladies. Some diabetes sufferers owe their lives to insulin produced from the glands of animals.

chapter

8

Some of the Builders

"There is properly no history, only biography." — *Emerson*

B. B. Paddock, editor of *The Fort Worth Democrat,* once explained the transformation of Fort Worth from a struggling frontier outpost to one of the state's great cities: "In the early days of this city there was among its citizenship a coterie of men, the like of which were never found in any community."

Many among that group now ~~SAMPLE BOOK~~ in historic Oakwood Cemetery near the Stockyard~~Not for Resale~~oneers rest on a hill, just across the Trinity River ~~SAMPLE/Not for Resale~~osing skyline of the city which they helped build.

It has been said that a walk through Oakwood is equivalent to a walk through the history of the city.

Here lie cattlemen Burk Burnett and W. T. Waggoner. And, in a mausoleum with a stained glass window picturing sunrise over the Mesa, rests another noted cattleman, John B. Slaughter.

Here, too, is John Peter Smith, and Maj. K. M. Van Zandt — alongside others of respected professions buried in Bartenders Row, or in a section reserved for bricklayers. Plots in Oakwood are owned by lodges, unions, Catholics and Protestants, Negroes and whites. Tracts are dedicated to both Confederate and Union soldiers.

One of the more impressive monuments in the Negro section, known as Trinity Cemetery, is that of "Gooseneck Bill" McDonald, a black banker and politician. Below the obelisk are three slabs of pink granite covering the graves of three of McDonald's family. McDonald's grave is, mysteriously, unmarked.

Even the participants in Fort Worth's most famous gunfight rest in Oakwood. Former city marshal "Longhair" Jim Courtwright was killed in that 1887 shootout at the White Elephant Saloon.

Courtwright's tombstone reads:

"U.S. Army Scout, U.S. Marshal, Frontiersman, Pioneer. Representative of a class of men, now passing from Texas. Who, whatever their faults, were types of that brave courageous manhood, which commands respect and admiration."

Luke Short, the saloon owner who killed Courtwright, died of natural causes a few years later. They are buried a stone's throw from each other.

There were no bridges across the Trinity when the Catholic section, known as Calvary, was set aside in 1880. Since all Catholic funerals were held downtown at St. Patrick's Cathedral, getting to Oakwood meant mourners must cross the river. The faint-hearted sometimes turned back. This led to a saying among early-day Catholics: "He is a good friend. He will follow you all the way across the river."

There always is the probability in naming names that many equally as worthy will be overlooked. This does not diminish any individual's contribution. However, some names stand out, and it is interesting to try to understand why.

Capt. E.M. Daggett, one of Fort Worth's first citizens, was a mountain of a man, both in physical size and in personal accomplishment. An Indian reportedly said of him that he was "Too big for a man, not big enough for a horse." Daggett was a military leader during the Mexican War and proved to be shrewd in business. Daggett served with Maj. Ripley Arnold during the Mexican War. Daggett then came to visit his friend shortly after Arnold established Fort Worth in 1849. Daggett was so impressed that he staked out large tracts and moved to Fort Worth from Shelby County in 1853 when the soldiers left. Daggett helped transform the abandoned fort into a town. He bought the cavalry stable and turned it into the town's first hotel. In 1856 he provided the county with its first jail. A year later he built and gave the county its first courthouse.

John Peter Smith was born in Owen County, Ky. He visited Fort Worth in 1853 and, fascinated with the area's natural beauty, decided to remain. He purchased land when it was cheap, and its appreciation brought him great wealth. Smith, a self-taught lawyer, opened Fort Worth's first school in 1854. He became involved in banking, was part owner of the city's first street railway, owned the gas works and a hotel. Smith could always be called upon to help in any advancement of the city. He donated 20 acres for the City Cemetery in 1879. The original tract now is part of the historically-treasured 62-acre Oakwood Cemetery.

Samuel Burk Burnett was among the first ranchers to embrace Fort Worth. He was born in 1849 in Missouri. The family came to Texas and settled in Denton County in 1857. Burnett grew up on a ranch and hired out in 1866 to drive cattle up the Chisholm Trail. He later became a trusted friend of Comanche Chief Quanah Parker and for years leased 300,000 acres of Indian land in southwest Oklahoma for grazing.

Burnett established the huge 6666 Ranch in King County in 1900. It still is a respected working ranch, famous for producing fine stock. Burnett was a pioneer in improving the Texas Longhorn breed. He became one of the largest landowners in Fort Worth and was active in promoting the city as a livestock center. He was a leading force in the establishment of and the success of the century-old Fort Worth Stock Show.

Maj. K.M. Van Zandt was born in 1836 in Tennessee. He commanded the 7th Texas Infantry Regiment and was captured at Chickamauga during the Civil War. He visited Forth Worth in 1865 and decided to move here. He dealt in cattle and real estate, then became part owner of the Tidball, Van Zandt & Co. Bank. Van Zandt was a part of just about every civic endeavor. He was elected - over his protest - to the Texas Legislature in 1873. Many times when the Trinity River was on a rise, visitors stranded on the west side of the river were invited to stay out the flood in his cabin. The cabin still stands on Crestline Road.

B.B. Paddock, editor of the *Democrat,* was outspoken and a driving force in just about every endeavor designed to benefit the city. He envisioned Fort Worth as a rail center and fought to see it happen. He saw Fort Worth as a great livestock market, and lived to see that dream come true as well.

Paddock was born in 1844 in Cleveland, Ohio and was reared in Wisconsin. He volunteered in the Confederate Army in 1861 and became the war's youngest commissioned officer at that time. Young Paddock trained as a lawyer, but he found the profession was not to his liking. He arrived in Fort Worth in 1872 and approached banker K.M. Van Zandt.

"What would you like to do?" Van Zandt asked.

"I would like to run a newspaper, sir," Paddock answered.

"Well, we have one here and we will give it to you if you will operate it," Van Zandt offered.

And operate it he did, with vision and energy.

Except for a convergence of cattle trails at Fort Worth, the frontier outpost had little to offer. Paddock made a difference.

He edited the *Democrat* for 10 years, then was managing editor of the *Fort Worth Gazette* for two years. He was responsible for the city's first water system, organized and promoted the world-famed Texas Spring Palace and, in 1885, was behind the building of the Fort Worth and Rio Grande Railway. He served five years as president and manager of the railroad.

Paddock was elected mayor of Fort Worth in 1892 and served four terms. His several books about the early days in Fort Worth and Texas are to this day treasured historic resources.

Maj. James J. Jarvis was born in 1831 in North Carolina and became a lawyer. One of the examiners for his bar fitness test was Abraham Lincoln. Jarvis came to Fort Worth in 1872, acquired land and established ranches in several surrounding counties. "His name is linked with that group of courageous and far-sighted men who actually made a city out of a frontier town," Paddock said. The Jarvis home ranch was located just north of the Fort Worth Stockyards.

W.T. Waggoner was born in 1852 in Hopkins County, the son of **Dan Waggoner,** a cattleman of prominence. The younger Waggoner was reared on his father's ranch near Decatur. He achieved the bulk of his wealth by the steady accumulation of land and livestock. Waggoner moved to Fort Worth from Vernon about the turn of the century and was active in promoting Fort Worth as a livestock center.

In 1903 he built the Fort Worth mansion, Thistle Hill, (now a popular tourist stop), as a wedding gift for his daughter, Electra. Waggoner entertained President Theodore Roosevelt in 1905 with a wolf hunt on his DDD Ranch, and the two became good friends. Waggoner left each of his three children 90,000 acres and 10,000 head of cattle. Oil was later discovered on these lands, further enriching the family fortune.

Amon Giles Carter, Sr. might be described as a 2nd generation Paddock. Like Paddock, Carter ran a newspaper, and, like Paddock, Carter never missed an opportunity to promote Fort Worth. Carter was born in 1879 in Wise County and, as a youth, sold chicken sandwiches to passengers on trains that stopped in Bowie. He came to Fort Worth in 1906 and became advertising manager of the new *Fort Worth Star*.

Because of his knowledge of that city, Carter scored a major newspaper scoop with an early account of the San Francisco earthquake. He copied a map that he had saved of San Francisco and, from memory of the city's buildings, described the devastation. Carter later became publisher of the newspaper, now *The Fort Worth Star-Telegram*.

Carter was a close friend of Will Rogers and of President Franklin D. Roosevelt, among others, and regularly entertained many other notables at his Shady Oak Ranch. Carter established WBAP (We Bring A Program) and, later, WBAP-TV television. He was an avid promoter of West Texas and of the livestock industry. Also like Paddock and his railroads, Carter promoted Fort Worth as an aerospace center and lived to see that dream become a reality. Carter enjoyed telling of drilling 90 dry holes before striking oil. In 1937 he discovered what was to become an oil-rich field in Gaines and Yoakum Counties. Before he died in 1955, Carter established the Amon Carter Foundation which since has donated millions of dollars to charities and for civic improvements, including the respected Amon Carter Museum.

chapter

9

And Still They Build

Paddock's coterie is still alive and well in Fort Worth.

Witness the wealthy Bass Brothers who have restored much of old downtown Fort Worth (Sundance Square) — at the same time building modern downtown skyscrapers which express an abiding faith in the future of Fort Worth.

Or witness Holt Hickman, a Fort Worth manufacturer so interested in preserving a piece of history that he simply bought the Fort Worth Stockyards in order that the site be preserved under local ownership.

Today's Fort Worth is a diversified city that still clings protectively to its past unique.

Fort Worth is home American Airlines, the Tandy Corporation, and Burlington-Northern Railroad. Tarrant County's modern-day cowboys build airplanes for Lockheed, helicopters for Bell-Textron and automobiles for General Motors.

Other major employers include Alcon Laboratories, D-FW Airport, IBM, Miller Brewing, Union Pacific Railroad, Hobbs Trailers and Motorola. Justin Industries operates Acme Brick and Justin Boots, which are known throughout the world.

Santa Fe Railroad is building a huge transfer hub on the west side of Alliance Airport, a new facility just north of the Stockyards, and Federal Express will build a $200 million hub there.

All this and, yet, the biggest annual event still is the century-old Fort Worth Stock Show. Cowboys and livestock still are first in the city's heart!

Fort Worth enjoys the best of all worlds. It draws on the vast resources of the Metroplex for economic stability, yet it retains the flavor of its heritage. The envied, easy going atmosphere belies the thriving economic machine that grinds out the present-day prosperity.

The future? Not to worry. Paddock's coterie already is at work on the next project.

The herds invading Fort Worth these days are tourists anxious to sample "Cowtown's" hospitality. It isn't a new phenomenon. The early-day trail herds were steered this way for the same reason. Cowboys liked the town.

Fort Worth merchants in 1909 ordered 2,400 felt hats for sale to those attending the cattlemen's convention in Fort Worth. One merchant predicted only one delegate in 10 would leave town without a new hat. And not cheap ones, either. Cattlemen were willing to pay for quality that could stand up to hard usage.

The city has continued to entertain all who appreciate its western heritage. In fact, the modern-day coterie seems determined to market Fort Worth as a primary destination for tourists.

In 1994 Hickman announced his intention to build a casino and 1,000-room hotel in the Fort Worth Stockyards if and when voters approve casino gambling in Texas. Hickman said the project would attract an additional 1.8 million visitors per year.

He said Stockyards development could make Fort Worth as attractive a destination as Rome or Paris. The prediction was met with skepticism from many, but there is a precedent.

In 1889, Fort Worth erected The Texas Spring Palace, an attraction so magnificent that newspapers everywhere lauded it. Paddock described it as "easily the most beautiful structure ever erected on earth." The 12 soaring, produce-covered towers and the entertainments inside were such a successful attraction that city fathers opened it again in 1890. Unfortunately, a fire broke out during the closing ball and it burned to the ground.

But, my! What a run it had!

Said *The Buffalo Express*: "The Texas Spring Palace will surpass the World's Fair in Paris. People who cannot go to Paris, France, this spring might do well to substitute a trip to Fort Worth."

The Texas Spring Palace was, in two words, a hoot!

It was as great a source of pride to local residents then as is the Fort Worth Stockyards National Historic District today.

Now that you know the history, let us in the next few pages tour the Stockyards and learn what all the fuss is about.

chapter
10 The Livestock Exchange

A guided tour can make your visit easier and even more meaning-ful. Tours are available for a small fee from the Visitors Center. Numbers in parentheses indicate the location of the site as found on the map on page 78.

A good spot to begin your tour — especially if it is a hot Texas day — is under a shade tree in front of the beautiful Livestock Exchange Building.

Livestock Exchange Building (1) t in 1902. This fine old building was the heart of the Stoc been described as "The Wall Street of the West." Ins any commission companies which served cattlemen pare a commission man to a pro football player's agen a rancher shipped his cattle to Fort Worth, it was the commi on man's job (as the agent) to negotiate the best price possible for consigned cattle. Also inside was a bank, a post office, five railroad offices, and three telegraph offices. Livestock prices at markets around the world were posted here. The building is comparatively quiet now, with various offices, a museum and the head-quarters of Lone Star Airlines inside. But imagine the hectic pace when as many as 5 million animals were traded each year. Tromping in and out of the building were cowboys, ranchers, commission men and cattle buyers.

The building can be appreciated for its architecture as well as its history. There was no air conditioning and very poor lighting when the Exchange Building was erected, so it has high ceilings to help keep it cool, and several skylights to illuminate the inside. Photographers seem to love the Spanish-style exterior.

Be sure to peek inside **Superior Livestock Auction** (2), a modern way to market cattle. Normally, to sell cattle, a rancher must round 'em up, haul 'em somewhere, and parade 'em around. The animals lose weight, and the rancher loses money. An even more modern way is to videotape the animals. Bi-monthly video auctions by satellite are scheduled by Superior. The auctioneer in the southwest corner of the room starts his sales pitch. A rancher in Montana, say, need only look at his TV, see animals that he wants, dial one of the operators manning the bank of telephones and begin bidding. Superior sells nearly a million head a year, in 38 states, Canada and Mexico.

Also inside is the free **Stockyards Museum** (3), operated by the North Fort Worth Historical Society. The museum has an excellent collection of Fort Worth Stockyards memorabilia, and Western and Indian Artifacts. Of particular interest is a collection from the Sesquicentennial Wagon Train that toured Texas in 1986. The museum also has a fine gift shop and is a good place to purchase Stockyards books and gifts.

Persons who wish to examine the building's design further may go to either the east or west wings and find a stairway to the second floor. Please respect the privacy of the offices in the building. You may leave by the rear door.

Auction Arena (4): To your right (east) is a more familiar auction arena. (Access is restricted to persons on escorted tours from the Visitor Center.) The auctioneer sits at a counter on a raised platform and animals are paraded in a pen below him. Bidders sit on rows of benches around the pen. There they can see the animals in which they are interested and signal their bids.

The Pens (5): Directly ahead (north) are the old cattle pens. Except for a few head of longhorns, the cattle pens normally are quiet now. In 1960 the pens were reduced from 80 acres to only seven acres remaining today. Use your imagination and you can still hear the thousands of cows out there, or hear the cowboys yelling. Maybe you can even imagine (ugh!) the smell! (If you visit immediately before the weekly hog auction, you won't have to imagine it!)

The Turnstile (6): To your right (enter a small alleyway behind the Auction Arena) then to your left find a century-old turnstile which allowed workers to enter the pens without opening a gate. Go through it if you wish. The small building beside it is the timekeeper's shack. The dim sign above the turnstile warns workers to put out their cigarettes before entering the yard. Fire starting in the hay and among the wooden pens was a constant threat.

The Brick: Note that all the cattle pens were paved with brick. More than 10 million bricks were required to pave the 2,600 pens in use when the Stockyards was in full operation. The object was to keep the animals clean and healthy and to deliver clean animals to the packing houses. You will see the name *Thurber* on many of the bricks. Thurber is now a tiny town about 70 miles west of Fort Worth. At the turn of the century its thriving economy was based on producing coal for steam engines and to fire kilns for making bricks.

Nearly all the bricks used in the Stockyards were made at Thurber. Time passed Thurber by, however. Railroads converted their steam engines to oil, and bricks fell out of favor as pavement. Thurber became a ghost town — though you may still pull off I-30 and read the historic marker near the remaining smoke stack of the old power plant.

The Cattlemen's Walk (7): An elevated walkway crosses over the cattle pens and provides a panoramic view of the Stockyards and of the remains of the old Swift & Co. and Armour & Co. meat packing plants.

Immediately to the west of the Livestock Exchange Building is the **Cowtown Coliseum** (8). Let's go there.

Exchange Avenue, 1904 - Note cupola atop the Livestock Exchange Building in this 1904 view of Exchange Avenue. In the foreground is an old wooden bridge over Marine Creek. Photo courtesy of Fort Worth Public Library.

Exchange Avenue, 1995- Cupola of the Livestock Exchange is visible behind the pecan tree, center, in this 1995 view. Marine Creek runs under the buildings erected on a "new" bridge built in 1910. Roof of Cowtown Coliseum is at top left.

chapter

11

The Cowtown Coliseum

The Cowtown Coliseum (8) is the home of the world's first indoor rodeo, and it still hosts rodeos and other events year 'round. The building is open most days. The Fort Worth Stock Show was born in 1896 along Marine Creek near the coliseum and was an immediate success. In 1907, it was decided to build the coliseum as a permanent home for the Stock Show. The coliseum was wanted so badly for the show in 1908 that this magnificent building was erected in only 88 working days. The Stock Show rodeo was held in the coliseum until 1942, when larger show facilities were built as the Will Rogers Coliseum. Notice the original wooden roof construction and the massive windows in Cowtown Coliseum. During daylight hours there is plenty of natural light inside to conduct almost any event.

In the front lobby is a statue of the great Comanche Chief Quanah Parker, once a frequent visitor to Fort Worth. The bronze was dedicated during an Indian Pow Wow in connection with the 1994 Chisholm Trail Round-up in the Stockyards.

Be sure to visit the Rodeo Shop inside the Coliseum. It contains a private collection of Western sculpture by Frederic Remington. You are free to browse here.

On the lawn in front of the coliseum is a magnificent bronze of **Bill Pickett** (9), the first bulldogger. This prominent piece of art by Lisa Perry shows Pickett throwing a longhorn. Pickett was the first black inducted into the Cowboy Hall of Fame. He appeared at the Cowtown Coliseum when it opened in 1908. Pickett was honored in 1994 with a 29-cent postage stamp. The stamp caused considerable embarrassment at the Post Office. The photo of Pickett's brother was used on the stamp by mistake. The stamps were recalled and the error was corrected, but not before some of the incorrect stamps were sold.

Rodeo Plaza is to the west of the Coliseum. It is a pedestrian walk which once served as a midway for the Stock Show. At the northwest corner of Exchange and Rodeo Plaza is a white, two-story building built on a bridge. (Marine Creek flows under the structure.) It originally was the **Stockyards National Bank** (10) but is now part of a western wear store. The bank vault is still operative and now houses some of the store's boots.

Along the plaza are some of the old Stock Show **Exhibit Barns** (11), which now contain individual shops. On the west side of the building are balconies from which one may view Marine Creek. The building once spanned the creek, but a flood in 1942 weakened the west half of the structure. Officials saved half the building by simply cutting it diagonally and demolishing the portion that spanned the creek.

Texas Gold (12), a massive bronze at the northeast corner of Stockyards Blvd. and Main, shows a cowboy headed up the trail with some longhorns. T.D. Kelsey sculptured this landmark piece, which is one of the world's largest bronze castings. This spot provides a good photo opportunity.

Now you are only a rope's throw from the world's largest honkey tonk, **Billy Bob's Texas** (13)!

Cowtown Coliseum - Eye-catching bronze of the first bulldogger, Bill Pickett, calls attention to Cowtown Coliseum, home of the world's first indoor rodeo.

chapter

12

Billy Bob's Texas

Billy Bob's Texas (13) is in a converted livestock exhibit building immediately north of Cowtown Coliseum. It is a "must see" for many visitors to the Stockyards.

The sprawling building — 127,000 square-feet, or almost three acres under roof — is known as The World's Biggest 'Honky Tonk.' It was built in 1936 for the Fort Worth Stock Show. By 1942 the Stock Show had outgrown this location and a new home for the exposition was built on the West Side. Billy Bob's had the building since 1981.

Billy Bob's accommodates customers and has 31 bar stations inside. Popular singers are booked into the huge saloon to entertain crowds.

Billy Bob's normally opens with a small cover charge each day at 11 a.m. (at noon on Sundays). Of particular interest inside is the bull riding arena. The club features live bull riding on Friday and Saturday nights. A "wall of fame" consists of dozens of concrete squares on which famous stars have pressed their handprints and scratched their autographs in cement.

A trip behind the scenes is offered with Stockyards tours from the Visitors Center and often includes a visit backstage, where many of today's major country-western stars have autographed the walls.

Now, let's retrace our steps along Rodeo Plaza, and return to Exchange Avenue.

The **Fort Worth Stockyards Sign** (14) spans Exchange Avenue. This is another photo opportunity. The structure marks the western entrance to the Fort Worth Stockyards Company property. It was originally built in 1910 and has become a Texas landmark.

35

Just east of the sign is the **Stockyards Hotel** (15), which was built in 1907 as the Stockyards Club. It was here that wealthy cattlemen stayed when they visited. The hotel was restored in 1984 and contains 52 rooms. Adjoining the hotel is **Booger Red's Saloon** (15). Bring your camera, because people at the bar sit on saddles and are cooled by belt-driven ceiling fans. See also a set of horns that measure nine feet from tip-to-tip. Also note the old tin ceiling, and the photo of the saloon's namesake.

Immediately to the west is the **Stockyards Drugstore** (16), opened in 1913 and the oldest continuously operated drugstore in the county.

Continue west along Exchange Avenue and make your own dis-coveries among the turn-of-the-century buildings. There is an old-time photo parlor, restaurants, saloons and a number of unusual shops to explore. On the south side of the street is **Miss Molly's Hotel** (17), once a bordello but converted now into a unique and popular eight room bed-and-breakfast "hotel." Cross Main Street again, walking east, and see the **Maverick** (18), an old-time saloon with ornate wooden bar, now better known for its fashionable western wear. The Maverick is in one of the oldest buildings along Exchange Ave. Just east of the Maverick is:

The White Elephant Saloon (19). It was at the White Elephant (then located downtown in the 300 block of Main Street) that Fort Worth had its most notorious gunfight. The saloon's owner, Luke Short, outdrew and killed popular "Longhair" Jim Courtwright, a former Fort Worth city marshal. The gunfight is re-enacted each February 8 in the street in front of the saloon. The saloon also is noted for its collection of hats and for the owner's collection of white elephants. The location has been used in movies and TV productions, including the television series, "Walker, Texas Ranger," starring Chuck Norris.

Marine Creek (20): A short alleyway just east of the White Elephant Saloon leads to an attractive overlook of Marine Creek, which has watered many a thirsty herd. Note how the buildings along Exchange Avenue have been built over the creek. Across the creek are more early-day buildings, including one that once housed a Wells Fargo Express Co. The wooden gates that were used when horses were stabled under the building are still in place.

Immediately to the east are the start of the **Horse and Mule Barns** (21). Let's look at 'em.

White Elephant - A famous gunfight occurred outside the White Elephant Saloon in 1887 and is re-enacted every year. The White Elephant has become a popular TV set and is known as "C.D.'s Bar" in the series *Walker, Texas Ranger*.

Back Stage - A tourist shot this photo in Billy Bob's Texas as your author talked with a group back stage. Walls of this often-private area are lined with autographs of numerous country western stars.

c h a p t e r

13

Horse and Mule Barns

The cavernous **Horse and Mule Barns** (21) were built on the site of the last Indian skirmish in Tarrant County, in 1869. These stables were large enough to house 3,000 horses and mules. They were rebuilt in 1912 after a fire destroyed the original wooden structures. The new fireproof barns were declared the finest stables in the world.

Come to **Mule Alley** (22), which separates the two strings of horse and mule barns. This was the world's busiest horse and mule trading center during World War I. The animals needed for the war in Europe. Sales jumped from about ~~~ year in 1914 to over 115,000 in 1917. By 1919, sales ~~~ back to about 60,000. In the west row of barns is ~~~

The National Cowgirl ~~~ of Fame (23), was persuaded in 1994 to move to the historic Fort Worth Stockyards. The Hall of Fame honors more than 100 women "who will live forever in your memory." It was established in 1975 at Hereford, Texas. Directors accepted a Fort Worth bid to move the collection into Barn D, directly across Exchange Avenue from Cowtown Coliseum. The coliseum has been the site of several recent National Cowgirl Finals Rodeos.

Directors subsequently decided to locate the Hall of Fame in a larger, newly-designed building near the Fort Worth Museum of Science and History in the Fort Worth Cultural District.

The Visitor Information Center (24) is immediately east of the horse and mule barns. The center offers information on area-wide attractions as well as on the Stockyards. Also sign up here for escorted, hour-long historic tours of the Stockyards. A mural inside the building catches the spirit of the Fort Worth Stockyards. It was painted by Stylle

Read and is a "must see." Behind the center is a carnival area and, for those who like Read's style, see excellent miniatures of western scenes that Read painted around the top of the merry-go-round. Continue to the east and see the:

Hog and Sheep Barns (25): These barns now are known as Stockyards Station, because an excursion steam train chugs right into the building about three times a day. The barns have been converted into a western shopping mall, but the original brick floors and some of the remaining gates and pens give it a special flavor. Spend some time exploring the unusual shops in this interesting building.

Hogs and sheep were unloaded along the east end of this building, where a number of railroad tracks once served the structure. Stroll to the east end of the building and see a feature that many visitors miss, a "Freeway for Animals."

The Stockyards was a big place. There was a huge slaughter house at each end of the yards; thus, a constant need to move animals from one end of the yards to the other. Crossing streets and opening the many gates proved inefficient. So look upon the two-way "freeway for animals," which runs the length of the yard. The "freeway" goes under all streets and ramps to give animals a non-stop journey from the north end of the yard to Swift & Co. at the south end, and from the south end of the yard to Armour & Co. at the north end. Offices were built over the busy "freeway" to enable workers to keep track of the movements.

Armour & Swift: On a small rise at the east end of Exchange Avenue are what remains of the Armour and Swift packing plants. **Armour and Co.** (26) was to the north and, though a large part of the plant has been razed, a food business operates in some of the remaining structures. **Swift & Co.** (27) was to the south and most of its buildings are gone. Of particular interest is the old Swift & Co. Headquarters, a striking, columned, historic building with stained glass windows. It now is a popular restaurant.

Branding Shed (28): Across Exchange Avenue is a small, tin shed that still has a sign that marks it as a branding shed and testing laboratory. This was for animals en route to a new ranch. Here the animals were tested for disease and marked with the new owner's brand. Many brands still are visible where the hot irons were tested on posts, fences or the side of the building. (This structure is generally not accessible to the public.)

The Brick Lot (29): Just west of the branding shed is a parking area known as "the brick lot." This area once was covered with cattle pens. The pens were removed and the century-old bricks now provide an acceptable parking surface.

In September 1994, Holt Hickman, the spark behind development and preservation of the Stockyards historic district, announced plans for a Luxury Hotel and Casino which would be built on "the brick lot" should Texas voters approve casino gambling. The hotel and casino and related convention and meeting facilities would be architecturally compatible with the historic Livestock Exchange Building next door.

Adjoining "the brick lot" immediately to the west is a rather new addition, a **Turntable** (30) on which the steam engine that pulls the popular "Tarantula" steam train is turned after each arrival. The 1896-model engine huffs and puffs and toots and is something every railroad buff will enjoy.

Those who wish may purchase tickets to ride the train to the 8th Avenue Yards (on the opposite side of town) and back. A longer trip originates in the historic City of Grapevine and brings visitors into the Stockyards by train.

Immediately to the west is the Livestock Exchange Building and your starting point. Now, put your imagination to work. Sense the clop of horses on brick, hear the deep-throated bawl coming from the cattle, hear the squeal of the hogs, visualize a happy cowboy who has just spent a month's wages on a new hat. Imagine the taste of a cowboy's chuck, experience the aroma, view the sign on old Theo's Cafe and wonder, "What are calf fries?"

14

There's Lots to Do in 'Cowtown!'

There's a good chance that you've spent a big chunk of your time in the Fort Worth Stockyards, but don't overlook other great attractions in Fort Worth.

A good place to start is at the **Fort Worth Convention and Visitors Bureau**. Knowledgeable volunteers will help plan your stay and point you in the right direction. There is an office in the Visitor Center at the Stockyards and another at 415 Throckmorton St. downtown. (Bus rides are free in the downtown area.)

Downtown Fort Worth is an [outdoor] [m]useum. The city had its beginnings in the few blocks [around the] historic **Tarrant County Courthouse**. The Cour[thouse was built] in 1895 at a cost of $300,000. Tarrant County taxpaye[rs were s]o angered by what they considered an extravagant expense tha[t th]ey threw out the entire group of commissioners in the next election. Completely restored in 1983 at a cost of $12 million, the building now is one of the city's treasures.

The **Original Fort** was built on the bluff immediately west of the Courthouse. The site is now occupied by several government buildings and Heritage Park. The picturesque park and overlook offers a panoramic view to the north. Use your imagination and picture what the first soldiers viewed from here. You will also see to the west a herd of cars parked along the Trinity River, where cattle once bedded down.

The people who park along the river ride the **M&O Subway** to their downtown jobs. The subway was an innovation of Marvin and Obie Leonard to bring customers right into the basement of their downtown Leonard Brothers Department Store. The free subway now serves the **Tandy Center**, which is on the site of the old store.

Fire Station No. 1, at 2nd and Commerce, now houses a museum, "150 Years of Fort Worth." Herds of cattle headed for the Chisholm Trail once plod down then-dusty Commerce Street in front of the fire station.

The Sid Richardson Collection of Western Art, 309 Main St., houses a fine collection of paintings by Frederic Remington and Charles M. Russell. The exhibit is located in a building surrounded by the shops and restaurants of Sundance Square.

At 3rd and Main the side of a three-story building is covered with **The Chisholm Trail Mural** that depicts a herd of longhorns trailing through town.

The Water Garden, at 15th and Commerce, is worth a visit. The cascading waterfall invites visitors to walk down into its innards, 10 a.m. to 10 p.m.

Immediately north of the Water Garden is the **Tarrant County Convention Center**, which occupies much of what once was known as Hell's Half Acre.

A dozen blocks west is the excellent **Cattleman's Museum**, 1301 W. 7th St. There's a lot of animation in this attraction that will teach you much about ranch life in the Southwest and about cattle rustling, past and present.

A sprawling area generally south of the 3300 block Camp Bowie is known as the **Cultural District**. Here are the Will Rogers Coliseum, Auditorium, Exhibits Hall, Equestrian Center and the many other structures that house the annual **Fort Worth Stock Show and Rodeo**.

Also in the Cultural District is the imposing **Amon Carter Museum**, 3501 Camp Bowie Blvd. The museum displays major works by 19th and 20th Century American artists, along with masterpieces by Remington and Russell.

Just to the south is the **Modern Art Museum of Fort Worth**, 1309 Montgomery, offering a collection of 20th Century art and sculpture along with special exhibits. Adjacent is the **William E. Scott Theater**.

The Fort Worth Museum of Science and History, 1501 Montgomery, is immediately to the south. This is Fort Worth's most popular visitor attraction. It houses the **Omni Theater** and the **Noble Planetarium**, and features history and science exhibits. Life-size sculptures of dinosaurs look on as kids search in sand for bones in the popular "Dino Dig."

The Kimball Art Museum, 3333 Camp Bowie, is also in the Cultural District. This world-class museum houses works of Rembrandt, Cezanne, Picasso and other greats and hosts shows and special exhibits of all the masters. There are countless works to dazzle your senses. The building itself, designed by Louis Kahn, is a work of art.

Casa Manana, 3220 Botanic Garden Drive, at the corner of Lancaster and University Drive is a domed theater-in-the-round that brings Broadway to Fort Worth. Drive south on University Drive, through beautiful park areas, and come to the **Botanic Garden**. The 114 acres includes a Rose Garden, a Japanese Garden, and the Conservatory.

A bit further south on University Drive, cross the Trinity River and come to **The Fort Worth Zoo**, now one of the great zoos in the world. Discover 4,500 exotic animals. See the outstanding World of Primates, the Asian Falls exhibits, and enjoy the hands-on diorama of frontier life in Texas.

By the river is the station for the longest **Miniature Train Ride** in the world. The train crosses the Trinity River on its own bridge and winds along the river and through the parks for five miles. It operates on a seasonal basis.

The Log Cabin Village, 2100 Log Cabin Village Lane, is a group of authentic 19th Century Texas cabins, with scheduled demonstrations of frontier life. Across University Drive from the zoo.

Just west of the Log Cabin Village is **Colonial Country Club**. It's world-class golf course is used for the annual Colonial National Invitation golf tournament.

Thistle Hill, 1509 Pennsylvania Ave., is a fine example of a cattle baron's mansion. It was built by W.T. Waggoner for his daughter's wedding present.

Well, Podnah, if by now you still have questions about Fort Worth and the West, you're just gonna have to visit.

Like the bumper sticker says, we don't hold it against you if you weren't born Texan — so long as you get here as quick as you can!

And Hoof - The first of 260 head of longhorns pass the Stockyards Hotel, left, as they depart in March 1995 on the Great American Trail Drive to Montana. View looks east on Exchange.

Pioneer Days - The front lawn of the Livestock Exchange Building becomes a pioneer village during the annual Pioneer Days Celebration each September.

chapter

15

Some Milestones

1836 — Battle of the Alamo, Feb. 23-March 6.
Battle of San Jacinto, April 21.
Texas becomes a Republic.

1840 — John Neely Bryan sets up a trading post at what is to become Dallas.

1841 — Gen. Edward H. Tarrant, for ~~whom~~ Tarrant County is named, and 69 militiamen, in ~~response to~~ Indian raids, attacks and routs 500 Indians ~~camped~~ ~~al~~ong Village Creek, near present-day Ar~~lington.~~ Jonathan Bir~~d establi~~shes community known as Bird's Fort, later renamed ~~Bi~~rdville.

1843 — Sam Houston spends a month at Bird's Fort as Indian chiefs gather for a peace parley. Indians agree to remain west of a line through what is now Fort Worth, thus Fort Worth's motto, "Where the West Begins."
Indian trader Ed Terrell sets up camp in a grove of trees at what is now Fort Worth, is captured by Indians, later escapes.

1845 — Texas becomes a state.

1849 — **Gold discovery in California attracts "49ers."**
Maj. Ripley Arnold establishes Camp Worth on June 6.
Camp Worth designated a fort on Nov. 14.

A comic one-shot battle routs the only Indian attack ever attempted against Fort Worth. Indians fled when soldiers fired a single cannon shot.

1850 — Major Arnold's wife and children arrive; two youngest die of cholera shortly after arrival.

1853 — Major Arnold is killed at Fort Graham by a fellow officer whom he had disciplined.
Fort Worth abandoned by soldiers on Sept. 17.

1856 — Fort Worth residents "steal" county seat from Birdville.

1858 — **Lincoln-Douglas debate in Illinois.**

1859 — Fort Worth to Jacksboro stage line starts.

1860 — Fort Worth interests agree to build a Courthouse, at no cost to taxpayers, in order to keep county seat.

1866 — Cattle drives start up Chisholm Trail.

1869 — Courthouse completed.

1871 — **Great Chicago Fire.**

1872 — Texas & Pacific completes track to Eagle Ford, six miles west of Dallas.
B. B. Paddock arrives to become editor of *The Fort Worth Democrat.*

1873 — Fort Worth incorporated March 1.
Financial panic in New York leaves completion of railroad in doubt. City's population dwindles overnight.

1875 — Citizens Construction Co. organizes to finish railroad.
Residents pledge money, materials and labor.
Courthouse burns.

1876 — **Custer's Last Stand.**
First railroad locomotive lumbers into Fort Worth at 11:23 a.m. on July 19.
First street railway, from Courthouse to depot (one mile), is "propelled by one mule something larger than a West Texas jackrabbit."

1877 — Daily mail, stagecoach from Forth Worth to Yuma, Ariz., starts. At 1,500 miles it is the longest stage run in the world. Trip takes 13 days.
First iced boxcar loaded with beef quarters leaves Fort Worth.
City employs first lamplighter to fire the gas lamps installed along city streets.

1879 — John Peter Smith gives land to establish the now-historic Oakwood Cemetery.

1881 — First telephone exchange opens with 40 customers.
Santa Fe Railroad enters Fort Worth.

1882 — Fort Worth & Denver Railroad enters Fort Worth.
John Peter Smith becomes mayor and is credited with putting city on sound footing: water system established, fire department reorganized, a paving program completed, sanitary sewers built and a public school system established.

1883 — **Brooklyn Bridge opens.**

1885 — City gets electric lights.
Foundation laid for St. Patrick's Cathedral, completed in 1892, is still in use.

1886 — Chief Yellow Bear dies when he blows out the gas light in his hotel room and goes to bed. His companion in the room, Chief Quanah Parker, survives.

1887 — "Longhair" Jim Courtwright is killed by Luke Short in gunfight outside White Elephant Saloon.
Union Stockyards (now Fort Worth Stockyards) chartered.

1889 — Spring Palace near intersection of present-day Lancaster & Main opens to world acclaim.

1890 — Al Hayne dies a hero as 7,000 persons escape a flash fire which destroys the Spring Palace. A monument in honor of Hayne stands at the site.

1892 — Boston entrepreneur Greenlief Simpson sees packed stockyards and becomes the catalyst that transforms Fort Worth into one of world's major livestock centers.

1893 — Fort Worth Stockyards Company chartered, later buys Union Stockyard.

1895 — Tarrant County's present Courthouse is erected.

1896 — First Stock Show held on banks of Marine Creek at Stockyards.

1900 — **Galveston hurricane claims 6,000 lives.**

1901 — Fort Worth Livestock Exchange incorporated.

1902 — Cornerstones laid for the new Armour and Swift packing plants.
North Fort Worth Town Site Co. purchases 1,200 acres and builds 1,040 homes near the Stockyards.

1903 — **Wright Brothers make first manned flight.**

1904 — Sam Rosen opens another huge tract of homes near the Stockyards known as Rosen Heights.

Some Milestones

1905 — President Theodore Roosevelt becomes first president to visit Fort Worth while in office.

1906 — *Fort Worth Star*, forerunner of today's *Star-Telegram*, is established.
John Philip Sousa performs at Greenwalls Opera House.

1908 — Cowtown Coliseum is completed in 88 working days.

1910 — Fort Worth Stockyards sign erected across Exchange Ave.

1911 — First airplane here sets down in a pasture west of downtown.

1916 — More than 3,000 Canadians and 5,000 American World War I pilots train at Hicks, Barron and Carruthers flying fields here.

1917 — A gusher on the McCleskey farm at Ranger touches off an oil boom destined to change Fort Worth's skyline.
Some 1,500 buildings go up on a 1,410-acre site along present-day Camp Bowie Blvd. to house and train the 36th Division for World War I.

1918 — World's first indoor rodeo staged in Cowtown Coliseum.

1920 — People pack coliseum to hear Enrico Caruso sing.

1936 — President Franklin D. Roosevelt opens Fort Worth's Frontier Centennial, staged by Billy Rose.

1941 — Ground broken for the mile-long Consolidated-Vultee bomber assembly plant (now Lockheed), which brings aerospace industry to Fort Worth.

1962 — Armour & Co. meat packing plant closes.

1971 — Swift meat packing plant closes.

1976 — Fort Worth Stockyards National Historic Site is designated.
Fort Worth Historical Society organized.

1981 — Billy Bob's Texas opens as "world's largest honkey tonk" in a former livestock exhibition barn at Stockyards.

1985 — Texas' Bi-Centennial Wagon Train arrives at Forth Worth Stockyards to end 3,000-mile, six-month trip around the state.

1992 — New Stockyards Visitor Center opens.
Stockyards Station takes shape.
Tarantula excursion train begins regular runs.

1994 — National Cowgirl Hall of Fame selects Fort Worth as its new home.
Holt Hickman buys Livestock Exchange Building and remaining cattle pens to keep them under local ownership.

1995 — Great American Cattle Drive departed Stockyards with a herd of longhorns bound for Miles City, Montana. The herd arrived there six months later.

1996 — Fort Worth Stock Show and Rodeo — which was born at the Stockyards in 1896 — celebrated its 100th anniversary.

1997 — Stockyards party hosts kickoff for huge Texas Motor Speedway.
First honorees named to Stockyards Trail of Fame.

chapter

16 The Stockyards Museum

Shortly after the Cowtown Coliseum had hosted its first event in 1908, a worker on Sept. 21 carefully screwed an electric light bulb into a backstage socket at the Palace Theater in downtown Fort Worth.

The bulb, after burning day and night for 30 years, was featured in Ripley's *Believe It or Not*. The still-burning bulb was moved to the Stockyards Museum after the theater was razed. As of September 1997, it still burned constantly, as it had for an incredible 89 years!

See it in a glass case in the northwest corner of the museum.

Visitors to the Stockyards would schedule an early visit to the museum, which is inside the historic Stockyards Exchange Building.

Here is a collection of photos and memorabilia of the huge Armour and Swift meat processing plants and of the busy stockyard which supplied them.

Greeting you as you walk in is the preserved head of a handsome Texas Longhorn, the animal that started it all.

Many exhibits are hung on some of the original gates that were used in the stockyard. The yard once had more than 2,600 pens.

Kids can try out a real saddle or sit on an authentic wagon seat.

In the Indian section, see a collection of arrowheads, along with Indian dress, weapons and ceremonial items. The hide of a rare albino buffalo is displayed here.

One popular exhibit is "The Bad Luck Wedding Dress," which was sewn in 1886. It is housed in its own glass case.

The Texas Bi-centennial wagon train finally arrived at the Fort Worth Stockyards in 1986 after a six-month, 3,000-mile trip around the state. The northwest section of the museum displays mementos presented at each stop along the way on that historic trek.

Be sure to marvel at the 230 samples of barbed wire on display, imagine yourself in the tin bath tub which once was a luxury on the frontier, and imagine a tune from the player piano.

The museum gift shop offers many unusual items, plus it has for sale an extensive selection of books about Fort Worth, the Stockyards, Texas and the West.

The non-profit museum is supported and operated by volunteers of the North Fort Worth Historical Society, who are happy to answer your questions. Admission is free. Donations for museum upkeep are appreciated.

17

Treaty of 1843

Most Texans know that Texas won its independence when the forces of Gen. Sam Houston in 1836 defeated the Mexican army of Gen. Santa Anna at San Jacinto.

Houston, elected first president of the new Republic of Texas, now faced an equally menacing enemy — the Indian.

Many adventurous pioneers from the United States, seeking to escape the financial panic of 1837, headed toward promise of a new life in the young Republic of Texas.

They found a frontier in North Texas that consisted of a few cabins scattered along stretching southward from the Red River. All areas line were dominated by hostile Indians.

Here were the Comanche, the Wichita, Taovayas, Tawakoni, Kichai, and Iscani tribes of the Wichita Confederacy.

Also, the Caddo, Ionie and Anadarko tribes.

The Deadose and Bidai who once lived in the lower valleys of the Trinity and Brazos Rivers also found their way into the northern section as Spanish and Anglo-American settlements took their hunting lands.

Other tribes were pushed into North Texas by United States expansion. These newcomers included the Coushatta, Kickapoo, Delaware, Shawnee, Choctaw, Chickasaw, Cherokee, Creek and Kiowa.

In 1837, Republic of Texas officials were notified that 500 warriors of the Wichita Confederation were hunting and roaming the prairies around the headwaters of the Trinity, Brazos and Colorado Rivers. The Indians were well-mounted and armed. They raided settlements, carried away children, and rustled cows and horses.

Other tribes added to the warrior total.

Another threat were some 8,000 Comanche warriors who ranged over vast areas of North and West Texas, moving their tepee villages every three days.

The young republic had a major problem in the 20,000 hostile Indians on the loose. The immediate need was to control the Indians in the rich area between the forks of the Trinity and the Red River.

Houston, first president of the republic, believed that Indians and whites should co-exist in a brotherhood of peace. His successor, Mirabeau B. Lamar, believed in a "big stick" policy. Lamar's attempted military solution not only was expensive but in reality worsened the problem.

Indian hostilities which resulted after 1839 almost depopulated North Texas. Half of all settlers abandoned the frontier and there were no newcomers.

To continue the war with the Indians would ensure that the rich lands of North Texas would remain a wilderness, Houston reasoned. Restore peace and the rich valleys of the upper Trinity and Brazos would explode with productive farms and towns.

Houston again was elected president of the republic and in 1842 set out to parley with all Indian tribes. The pow wow finally was scheduled at tiny Bird's Fort just east of present-day Fort Worth.

On hand were chiefs of the Delaware, Chickasaw, Waco, Tawakoni, Kichai, Caddo, Anadarko, Ionie, Biloxie and Cherokee tribes. Comanches chose not to attend.

What resulted was a treaty of tremendous consequence.

The most significant point of agreement was one in which the Indians agreed to a line that would divide Texas in two parts — the red man's hunting ground to the west and white man's lands to the east.

Negotiators promised to build a line of trading houses to which Indians could bring their hides, pelts, buffalo robes and tallow to trade for needed goods.

The Treaty of 1843 was the tool of peace that helped the reaches of the upper Trinity emerge from wilderness to prosperous habitation.

The line, drawn from present day Fort Worth, to Menard, to San Antonio brought as much order to the frontier as any action of that time could do. The trading houses were to be established at the juncture of the Clear Fork of the Trinity (present site of Fort Worth), at Comanche Peak near Granbury, and on the San Saba River near the old Spanish mission in Menard County.

After Texas became a state, the United States government took on the job of Indian defense and adopted the same line of demarcation established by the Treaty of 1843. Indians were to stay west of the line through Fort Worth.

Fort Worth in reality became the city "Where the West Begins."

Though the Treaty of 1843 brought relative peace, Indian depredations continued for another 30 years — until the buffalo were decimated in the 1870s. This finally forced Indians onto reservations.

The great Comanche chief Quanah Parker, who reigned over the Texas Panhandle, led his warriors in spirited fights to protect their hunting grounds, but when the buffalo were gone, Quanah taught the Comanches to profit through cooperation with the white man. However, Indian culture remains intact.

One of the more popular features of the annual Chisholm Trail Round-up held in the Stockyards each June is the colorful Indian Pow-Wow staged in Cowtown Coliseum.

18

Cattle Brands

On the south wall of Stockyards Station, burned into the fence,are markings designed to show ownership of cattle, horses and mules.

Branding is an ancient practice of identifying an animal by burning a distinctive mark on its hide. Branding can be traced to ancient Greece and to the Roman Empire. It has been used in Texas since 1821.

On the open ranges of the frontier, cattle mixed freely with animals of other owners. Unfenced ranges made branding as necessary as naming your children.

The first brands were rather simple, burned into the hides with several applications of "dotting irons." The irons came in three basic shapes, a simple bar a few inches long, a capital *C* and a small *c*.

With the bar and capital *C* irons, you might make a *D*.

Use two small *c*'s to make an *o*. With this and a bar you might make one of the most recognized brands in Texas, the "Four Sixes," or 6666.

The dotting irons soon gave way to irons which contained the whole brand. Now the brand could be applied in one operation.

Ranchers on open ranges participated in general spring and fall roundups to sort animals by brand and to mark new calves.

When animals were sold, they generally got an extra brand — that of the new owner.

Several ranchers often would go in together to make up a trail herd of 2,000 or so animals. These cattle were given yet another marking, a trail brand. Should there be strays or a stampede, the animals of a particular trail herd could easily be identified and the herd reestablished.

Brands are used today, along with distinctive ear marks, to establish proof of ownership. Brand inspectors of the Southwestern Cattle Raisers Association regularly check animals that are being traded for proper ownership.

The thousands of brands registered in Texas serve to identify, of course, but they also are a reflection of the rancher's practicality, ingenuity, or sense of humor.

A visit to The Texas and Southwest Cattle Raisers Association's Cattleman's Museum in Fort Worth will graphically show how cattle branding and work of the association's tough brand inspectors have rendered cattle rustling today as truly a crime that doesn't pay. It is a phenomenal record considering there are more than 14 million head of cattle in Texas today.

Sample Brands and Their Meanings

When investors built Texas' state capitol in Austin and were paid with 3 million acres in the Texas Panhandle, they set about thinking up an appropriate brand for the huge spread. Since the ranch covered parts of 10 counties, they made it the "Ten in Texas," or:

XIT

It is said that Burk Burnett won part of his great ranch at Guthrie in a poker game. The famed hand became his brand, "Four Sixes:"

6666

Another rancher obviously described his method of staying in business on the "I Bor-row:"

I−O

On this one, a little girl once asked, "Who put all the valentines on the cattle?"

The "running W" identifies the 24,000 cows on the vast King Ranch at Kingsville:

UV

Cattle on the Guthrie's 172,000-acre well-managed Pitchfork Ranch bear this descriptive brand:

山

The Spade Ranch at Lubbock registered its brand in 1880:

o−▭

The "JA" worked in 1876 for John Adair and the revered Charles Goodnight:

A

Former Texas Governor Dolph Briscoe of Uvalde used a simple "9" on his 16,500 cows:

Former Gov. Price Daniel used the "HR":

Gov. John Connally used a scrawled "JN":

Dan Waggoner's brand at Vernon was the "reverse D," registered in 1850:

Or how about the "frying pan"?

Or "Bar-B-Que"?

Or "Too Fat"?

Or "Walking T"?

chapter

19

The Texas Longhorn

There is no symbol that stirs up images of a day now gone than that of a head-on view of a handsome Texas Longhorn.

Millions of longhorn cattle once roamed the unfenced open ranges of Texas, yet they once were closer to extinction than even the buffalo.

Christopher Columbus is said to have brought the seed for the vast Texas Longhorn herds from Spain on his second voyage to the New World in 1493, landing the Spanish cattle at Santa Domingo. Some of these cattle were introduced into Mexico 〈...〉.

Explorers and early settlers br〈...〉 the cattle into Texas. Many cows were left on their 〈...〉ved through adaptation to sparse grasslands and sc〈...〉ey became hardy, disease-resistant, fertile and long-live〈...〉 ate and thrived on whatever forage was at hand.

Men returning home from the Civil War found economic salvation in the millions of longhorns roaming the open ranges. These animals were almost worthless in Texas, but would bring a good price "up-north."

Fort Worth became an important stop on the famed Chisholm Trail. It was the last bit of civilization before the final 400-mile drive north to the nearest railroad in Kansas. An estimated 10 million Texas cattle were trailed to northern markets between 1866 and 1892.

Barbed wire, railroads and new breeds of beef were the downfall of the longhorn. Open ranges were fenced, ranchers began building their herds around imported breeds, and the spread of railroads was an alternative to trail drives for transporting less hardy breeds.

The number of Texas Longhorns dwindled to a point near extinction. The U.S. government appropriated $3,000 in 1927 to acquire a herd of longhorns for preservation.

Forest Service employees traveled 5,000 miles and could find only 23 head. There animals became the foundation stock for the federal herd at the Wichita Mountains National Wildlife Refuge in Cache, Oklahoma. Here was the seed for today's longhorn population.

The Texas Longhorn Breeders Association of America, now headquartered in the Fort Worth Stockyards National Historic District, today has 4,000 members and has registered over 250,000 longhorns.

An association publication states: "The same characteristics that the Texas Longhorn developed through the years of neglect are in demand by the cattlemen of the twentieth century — calving ease, fertility, disease resistance and longevity." Breeders say the longhorn produces the kind of lean beef that is in demand today.

That's a far piece from the wild, stampeding, trail-toughened herds of the past.

20

Barbed Wire

Joseph Glidden, an Illinois farmer, is credited with inventing barbed wire in 1874. His aim was to keep dogs out of his wife's flower garden.

When barbed wire arrived in Texas, John "Bet-a-Million" Gates built a corral in downtown San Antonio, put longhorns inside and bet all comers that the cows wouldn't get out.

The bit of showmanship resulted in more orders than could be filled. A flood of patents were issued as entrepreneurs quickly devised more than 1,000 designs of barbed wire.

In 1875 came the Fentress "Diamond" and Haish's "S Barb."

In 1876, Merrill's "Tack" and others.

In 1878 came Reynolds' "Necktie," Havenhill's "Y Barb" and Upham's "Side S."

Then there was Kelly's "Diamond Point," Hodge's "Spur," Allis' "Barbless," the "Sawtooth Ribbon," the "Flemish 4 Braid," the "Snail Barb" and the "Bent Washer."

The first major fences were placed more to keep cattle out of a pasture than to keep them in. In the severe winter of 1880, thousands of cattle drifted hundreds of miles south from Colorado, Kansas and Nebraska.

Grass along the Canadian and Red River was eaten clean by the unwelcome intruders. Cooperating cattlemen in 1882 built a 200-mile "drift" fence across the Texas Panhandle to deny grass to cattle drifting down from the north.

Barbed Wire

Texas trail-blazer and rancher Charles Goodnight, who early on established the famed JA Ranch in the Palo Duro Canyon, strung the first barbed wire in the Panhandle — a short line across the canyon to contain his pure bred herd.

Ten drivers with a 30-wagon supply train delivered the 67 miles of barbed wire, among other needs, to Goodnight's "home ranch" in 1880.

Barbed wire generally was hated by free-grass ranchers as it fenced off what once were open grasslands and denied access to precious water. Fences also hampered cowboys attempting to drive cattle cross country.

Fence cutting became common and disputes sometimes resulted in loss of life. Fence cutting finally was made a felony offense in Texas.

For all the hatred of fencing, barbed wire contributed mightily to the robust health of the cattle industry in Texas. Ranchers with secure pastures now controlled breeding and quickly improved their herds.

The Fort Worth Stockyards Museum has an excellent documented display of many designs of wire.

21

Trail of Fame

Visitors will notice as they stroll around the Stockyards the markers embedded in sidewalks. The plaques constitute the Texas Trail of Fame, a program recognizing persons who "earned their spurs" through contributions to the heritage of the West.

An initial 16 honorees were named in May, 1997, and an additional dozen in October 1998. Plans were to honor others periodically. Those honored through January 1999 and location of the markers were:

Stephen F. Austin, Marker L___ **eo Plaza** — Born in Virginia and raised in Missouri ____ ___ known as "The Father of Texas." His own father, M___ ___nt from Mexico to establish a colony of 300 anglos in ___ ___ en Moses Austin died, his son took over and established the fi___ Texas colony at San Felipe de Austin in 1821. He wanted Texas as a state within Mexico. When the Mexican government imposed objectionable policies on the colony, he went to Mexico City to plead his case before Santa Anna. He was jailed, then released, and became a leader in the new Texas republic.

Gene Autry, Marker Location: Front of Billy Bob's Texas — Born at Tioga, north of Fort Worth, the young Autry hankered to be a professional baseball player and did play in a semipro league. However, his work as a singer with the Fields Brothers Marvelous Medicine Show won him a spot on The Oklahoma Yodeling Cowboy radio show. He was signed by Republic Pictures in 1934, starred in 88 movies, 95 half-hour television programs, and wrote more than 250 songs.

S.B. Burk Burnett, Marker Location: South entrance to Cowtown Coliseum — Born Jan. 1, 1849 — the year that Fort Worth was established — Burnett at 15 was one of the first cowboys to push longhorns up the Chisholm Trial. By the following year, the 16-year-old cowboy was a trail boss. Burnett began assembling ranches in 1871, including the famed 6666 Ranch at Guthrie. It is said the Four Sixes Ranch got its name when Burnett won part of the land by holding four sixes in a poker game. Discovery of oil increased Burnett's wealth. He died June 27, 1922. (See more on Burnett on page 26.)

Amon G. Carter, Sr., Marker Location: Entrance to Stockyards Visitor Center — The publisher of the *Fort Worth Star-Telegram* was the most widely-known promoter of Fort Worth and of West Texas in the 20th Century. He was a major force in establishment of Big Bend National Park and of Texas Tech University. Carter was born in Bowie, Dec. 11, 1879. Carter and some friends were at the Fort Worth Stockyards in 1905 to assess the commercial value of burning cow chips for energy. The group agreed, instead, to start a newspaper, The *Fort Worth Star*, forerunner of the *Fort Worth Star-Telegram*. They shook hands over a pile of smoldering cow dung to establish what would become a great newspaper. They decided against investing in cow chips as fuel. Too smelly! Carter died June 23, 1955. (See more on Carter on page 28.)

Dale Evans, Marker Location: Rodeo Plaza near Cowtown Coliseum — Born Oct. 31, 1912 at Uvalde. She came to be known as "America's Cowgirl." When Republic Pictures teamed her with Roy Rogers, she found a husband as well as stardom. She and Roy made 26 western movies together and then starred in their own radio and television series. She and Roy adopted children from Scotland and Korea, among other places. Then with 30 grandchildren, Dale was in 1967 named California Mother of the Year. She was named Texas Woman of the year in 1970. She also is honored in the National Cowgirl Hall of Fame.

Charles Goodnight, Marker Location: Across Exchange Ave. from Cowtown Coliseum — Anyone who has seen the television miniseries *Lonesome Dove* or who has read Larry McMurtry's book which inspired the movie can trace many parallels in the lives of

Charles Goodnight and McMurtry's fictional Woodrow F. Call. Both were former Texas Rangers, both blazed new cattle trails, and both were demanding and loyal and unforgiving of weakness. Both honored death-bed promises to haul a friend's body hundreds of miles so the body could be buried as wished. Goodnight was born in Missouri March 5, 1836, and in the next 93 years became a living legend in Texas and the West. He settled in North Texas as a young man and during the Civil War was a scout and tracker for the Texas Rangers protecting the Texas border. Goodnight and Oliver Loving laid out the imaginative Goodnight-Loving Trail over which herds of longhorns from Texas were delivered to the gold fields of Colorado. Goodnight later established the famed JA Ranch in the Panhandle's Palo Duro Canyon. He once had oversight of 1.3 million acres. He died in 1929.

Zane Grey, Marker Location: Southeast corner of Main and Exchange — More than 100 movies have been made based on the writings of Zane Grey. Born in Zanesville, Ohio, Grey as a youth was interested in stories of western expansion. He gave up a career in dentistry to begin a writing career. He went west in 1907 and was thrilled by its endless horizons. Grey, who died at age 67, wrote more than 90 novels. Two-thirds of them were westerns.

Sam Houston, Marker Location: Rodeo Plaza — What a man! What an enigma! Sometimes Texas' greatest hero, sometimes the state's biggest heel. But what a story! He served at various times as governor of two different states, U.S. senator from two different states, and as president of the Republic of Texas. Between jobs, he drank heavily and opted for a self-imposed exile among the Cherokee Indians. Houston was born March 2, 1793, on a Virginia plantation. He came to Texas in 1832 and, partly because he had been a general back in Tennessee, was named commander-in-chief of military forces during Texas' fight for independence. He endured criticism as he led his troops on a seemingly-endless retreat before the pursuing Mexican army following the battle of the Alamo. The criticism turned to adoration following Houston's stunning defeat of Mexican general Santa Anna at the Battle of San Jacinto, assuring Texas independence. Houston died in 1863.

Bose Ikard, Marker Location: Across Exchange Ave. from Cowtown Coliseum — Another whose life is mirrored in *Lonesome*

Dove, as the talented and respected black cowboy Josh Deets. Ikard was born a slave in Mississippi in July 1843. He became one of Texas' foremost cowboys and Indian fighters. He came to Texas with his owner, Dr. Milton Ikard, who settled in Parker County. Ikard became free after the Civil War and hired on to drive longhorns to New Mexico and Colorado over the Goodnight-Loving Trail. At Ikard's death and burial in Weatherford, Charles Goodnight placed a marker which read: "Bose Ikard served with me four years on the Goodnight-Loving Trail, never shirked a duty or disobeyed an order, rode with me in many stampedes, participated in three engagements with Comanches, splendid behavior."

John Justin Jr., Marker Location: Near White Front Western Store — Justin boots were a standard of the West even before John Justin Jr. was born Jan. 27, 1917. Justin's grandfather, Herman, came to Texas from Indiana in 1877 and apprenticed himself to a cobbler in Gainesville. Two years later he moved to Spanish Fort, a settlement where the Chisholm Trail crossed the Red River. Many of the cowboys trailing herds stopped at his sign. Justin hand-fitted each cowboy and developed a stronger pattern of stitching. Satisfied cowboys ordered boots going up the trail and picked them up on the way home. Justin prospered. The firm moved to Fort Worth in 1925. John Justin Jr. has ably carried on the tradition and Justin boots — in 400 styles — remains the reason why the word "Justins" is an acceptable synonym for "boots."

Richard King, Marker Location: South side of Exchange in front of Mule Barn – The King Ranch on the Texas Gulf coast is so large and isolated that it boasts its own unique culture. The 285,000-acre spread extends into eight counties and is home to 85,000 head of cattle and 3,000 fine horses. Richard King, born in New York City, July 10, 1824, was a riverboat pilot by the time he was 16. He used these earnings to begin acquiring land between the Nueces and Rio Grande Rivers, building the vast King Ranch. He went to Mexico in 1854 and persuaded the population of an entire village to come with him to Texas to work the ranch. Many descendants of those original cowhands continue to work the ranch today. From 1869 to 1884, more than 100,000 longhorns from the ranch were driven up the Chisholm Trail to market. The

King Ranch for this reason is known as the birthplace of American ranching. King died in 1885.

Oliver Loving, Marker Location: Across Exchange Avenue from Cowtown Coliseum — Born in Kentucky Dec. 4, 1812, Loving's 55 years of life was fictionalized in the television mini-series *Lonesome Dove* as Agustus McCrae. In real life Loving was the catalyst that brought on the cattle drive era. He, his wife and nine children gave up farming in Kentucky and moved to Texas in 1855. Two years later Loving figured he could find a profitable market by driving cattle to Illinois along the Indian-blazed Shawnee Trail. The drive was profitable. During the Civil War Loving trailed cattle to Mississippi to feed Confederates. It was after the Civil War that he teamed with Charles Goodnight to blaze the Goodnight-Loving Trail to Fort Sumner, New Mexico, then on to Denver. They established a New Mexico Ranch even as they continued to drive longhorns over the trail. The end of the partnership came in 1867. Loving was wounded in an attack by Indians. He made his way to Fort Sumner, but gangrene had spread from the wound. As he lay dying, Loving told Goodnight he wanted to go home. Goodnight promised to take him and, true to his word, later loaded the body of his friend in a wagon and hauled it several hundred miles to be buried in Weatherford.

Tad Lucas, Marker Location: East of Coliseum Ticket Office — She was born Barbara Inez Barnes Sept. 1, 1902 in Nebraska, the youngest of 24 children, and came to be known as "Rodeo's First Lady." She rode almost before she could walk and by age 13 was winning cash prizes riding wild calves. Tad, known as "Tadpole," routinely performed riding tricks that others wouldn't attempt — such as changing sides of a running horse by crawling under its belly. For eight years she was all-around cowgirl and world champion woman trick rider in Madison Square Garden. She has been honored by the National Cowgirl Hall of Fame, the National Cowboy Hall of Fame, and the Professional Cowboys Association. She married champion steer wrestler and bronc rider Buck Lucas in 1924 and they moved to Fort Worth. A daughter, Mitzi, became a champion trick rider in her own right. Tad Lucas died Feb. 23, 1990.

Watt Matthews, Marker Location: Entrance to Livestock Exchange Building — This giant among ranchers can be described as "a cowboy's cowboy." Matthews was born Feb. 1, 1899 and, except for his education at Princeton, lived his entire life on his beloved Lambshead Ranch near Albany. He dressed as a working cowboy and for much of his life slept in the bunkhouse with the ranch hands. Matthews' father, John Alexander Matthews, began putting together the 40,000-acre Lambshead Ranch in the 1870s. Watt Matthews, a ranch manager, enlarged the Hereford herd, brought in and re-bred longhorns and worked with Shorthorns. Lambshead cattle came to be known for purity of breeding. But the admirable charm of Watt Matthews was his and his family's devotion to the land and to love of ranching. *Interwoven: A Pioneer Chronicle*, written by Matthews' mother, Sallie Ann, became basis for the story of Albany's famed Fort Griffin Fandangle. Watt Matthews died April 13, 1997 and was buried on the ranch in a plain pine box.

Jose Antonio Navarro, Marker Location: Southwest corner of Main and Exchange Ave. — A descendent of Spanish nobility, he was convinced that Texans had a destiny worth following. As an elected representative to the state of Texas in Mexico's National Congress, Navarro represented the cause of Texans and sided with them in their arguments with the government of Santa Anna during the turbulent 1834-36 period. When war came, Navarro joined other delegates from San Antonio at Washington-on-the-Brazos to sign the Texas Declaration of Independence. A lawyer by training, Navarro helped write a new constitution for the Republic of Texas and was elected to the congress of the new republic. Navarro promoted American statehood and voted for annexation of Texas. He also helped draft a new state constitution. Navarro was born in San Antonio Feb. 17, 1795 and died Jan. 13, 1871. Texas' Navarro County was named in his honor.

Annie Oakley, Marker Location: In front of Cowtown Coliseum — Her real name was Phoebe Moses. Her shooting ability surfaced early. Phoebe was born in Ohio and, at age 7, she fired her father's Kentucky rifle for the first time. By the time she was 12 she could shoot the head off a running quail. In later life, as Annie Oakley, she performed with Chief Sitting Bull in Buffalo Bill Cody's Wild West Show. She was equally good with rifle or pistol. Chief Sitting Bull called her "Little Miss Sure Shot." Irving Berlin's musical *Annie Get Your Gun* was based on her life. She died Nov. 2, 1926.

Quanah Parker, Marker Location: Near the White Elephant Saloon — Last of the great Comanche Indian Chiefs, Quanah was both a "hawk" and a "dove." He fought the white man when it served the purposes of his people, but he took up the ways of the white man when that seemed in their best interest. Even more famous than Quanah was his mother, Cynthia Ann Parker, a white girl taken captive by Comanches in 1836. She was 9. Cynthia accepted life with the Indians and eventually married Chief Peta Nocona. One of their three children, born about 1845, was Quanah. He was chief of the Quahadi Comanches and ruled the Llano Estacado in the Texas Panhandle. Never defeated militarily, the Comanches finally were forced onto an Oklahoma reservation by decimation of the buffalo. Quanah then embraced many of the white man's ways and urged his people to do so. Quanah amassed a fortune in cattle and land. He justified the lease of Oklahoma Indian lands to white ranchers. He pointed out the white man's cattle would graze the lands anyhow. Indians might as well be paid for it. Quanah and members of his tribe appeared in Cowtown Coliseum shortly before his death Feb. 23, 1911.

Bill Pickett, Marker Location: West of Coliseum Ticket Office — One of the more beautiful western bronzes anywhere commands the attention of Stockyards visitors outside Cowtown Coliseum. It depicts the famous black cowboy, Bill Pickett, wrestling a longhorn steer. The rodeo event which came to be known as a bulldogging was invented by Pickett, who was born Dec. 5, 1870. Pickett said he got the idea for steer wrestling by watching dogs in his hometown of Taylor bite a steer's lip to drag the 1,000-pound animal to the ground. Pickett tried it and soon was the talk of Texas. Pickett became star of the 101 Ranch Wild West Show and thrilled spectators everywhere, including at Cowtown Coliseum. Pickett was the first black inductee of the National Rodeo Hall of Fame. He is in the Pro Rodeo Hall of Fame and the Museum of the American Cowboy. Pickett was fatally injured April 2, 1932, when kicked in the head by a horse on the 101 Ranch in Oklahoma.

Fredrick Remington, Marker Location: East Exchange east of the Tarantula Train track — Few artists have made such an impact on the heritage of the American West. Remington's sketches, paintings and sculptures bring to life the stories of the frontier. Remington was born in New York, the son of a cavalry colonel and Civil War commander. He became a master at painting charging horses and soldiers, illustrating Indian battles and recording the toughness of life on the frontier. Remington is acknowledged as one of the primary sources of documentation of events and people that settled the American West. Fort Worth's Richardson and Amon Carter Museums own many of his treasured works. Remington died Dec. 26, 1909.

Sid W. Richardson, Marker Location: Entrance to Livestock Exchange Building — Sid Richardson was exactly what you think a Texan wildcat oilman should be — rich one day, broke the next — until he got too rich to go broke. Richardson was born April 25, 1891 in East Texas. After dealing in cattle for a while, Richardson moved to Fort Worth to make his fortune in oil. He struck it rich in 1935 with discovery of the vast Keystone field in West Texas. The bonanza was the keystone to a business empire that included ranching, radio networks and railroads. Much of his fortune was placed in a foundation which has given millions of dollars to Texas hospitals and colleges. The Richardson Museum in downtown Fort Worth preserves his valuable collection of western art. Richardson died Sept. 30, 1959.

Roy Rogers, Marker Location: Rodeo Plaza near Cowtown Coliseum — Hollywood's "King of the Cowboys" made more than 100 western movies during his career. He was born as Leonard Slye, Nov. 5, 1911, in Ohio. In 1930 he went to California and worked at odd jobs while trying to break into show business. He met Bob Nolan and Tim Spencer, and they formed the Pioneer Trio, which later became the Sons of the Pioneers. The group's *Tumbling Tumbleweeds* and *Cool Water* have become classics. Republic Pictures changed Slye's name in 1938 to Roy Rogers and began starring him as Republic's answer to the popular Gene Autry. Both went on to great fame. Rogers' first wife died in 1946 and he married his new co-star Dale Evans. Their signature song, *Happy Trails*, also has become a classic.

Will Rogers, Marker Location: Near the Tarantula Train tracks outside Stockyards Station — No news of an accidental death has shocked Fort Worth more than a news bulletin on Aug. 15, 1935. The flash reported that an airplane crash in Alaska had taken the lives of Will Rogers and Wiley Post. Rogers was the most loved man in America at the time, and was loved even more in Fort Worth, for "Cowtown" was his second home. Rogers was in Fort Worth shortly before he flew off to his death. Rogers was born on a ranch near

Claremore, Oklahoma, Nov. 4, 1879. He ran away from home as a boy, worked on a ranch in the Texas Panhandle, then accompanied a shipload of cattle to Argentina. He worked his way to South Africa and joined a wild west circus. Rogers became skilled at rope tricks. By 1905 he was performing in Madison Square Garden where he was noticed by Broadway producers. Rogers began to add humorous comment to his work with the rope and soon was starring in the Ziegfield Follies. He did movies, wrote books and wrote a column syndicated to 300 newspapers. Rogers was a close friend of *Fort Worth Star-Telegram* publisher Amon Carter and he liked the laid-back atmosphere in Fort Worth. The city's Will Rogers Coliseum and Auditorium are named in his memory. A statue of Rogers sitting on his horse, Soapsuds, stands in front of the complex.

George W. Saunders, Marker Location: In front of Livestock Exchange Building — Born in Gonzales County Feb. 12, 1854, George Washington Saunders had cattle in his blood. By 1871, the 17-year-old was driving cattle up the trails to Kansas and other northern markets. After moving to San Antonio, Saunders entered the business of trading cattle. By 1910, the George W. Saunders Livestock-Commission Company had offices in San Antonio, Kansas City, St. Louis and in the Fort Worth Livestock Exchange building. The company, when it dissolved in 1958, was the oldest livestock commission firm operating continuously under the same name in Texas. Saunders had a hand in publication of the valuable historic resource book *Trail Drivers of Texas*. Saunders also was instrumental in placing in San Antonio the Trail Drivers Monument which honors the memory of 35,000 drovers who went up the trail. The Fort Worth Stockyards honors the Saunders family with a historical marker in Saunders Park along Marine Creek, which flows under Exchange Ave.

Juan Seguin, Marker Location: Northwest corner of Main and Exchange Ave. — Juan Seguin, born in San Antonio Oct. 27, 1806, was both a proud Mexican and Tejano. He was a critic of Santa Anna and, when he had to choose between Texas and Mexico, he threw in with Texas. He served at the Alamo with Col. William B. Travis and survived because he was sent for reinforcements shortly before the Alamo was overrun. Seguin was a captain in the Texas army and, with his squad, served as scout and rear guard for Sam Houston's troops. He became a hero of the Battle of San Jacinto. Elected to the Texas Senate, Seguin was the only Mexican-Texan to hold that office. Seguin later returned to Mexico and was forced to fight against the United States in the U.S.-Mexican War. He returned to Texas after that war ended.

C.C. Slaughter, Marker Location: In front of Livestock Exchange Building — He already was working cattle at age 12. At 17 he was trading cattle. Born in Sabine County Feb. 9, 1837, Christopher Columbus Slaughter, in quest of better quality animals, persuaded his father to move west. The family settled near Palo Pinto County. Slaughter in 1871 brought Shorthorn bulls from Kentucky to breed a herd of good heifers and thus became one of the pioneers in improving Texas Longhorns. He eventually established the Long S Ranch on the headwaters of the Colorado River and once owned more than a million acres and 40,000 head of cattle. He was a former Texas Ranger. Slaughter was a force in founding the Texas Southwestern Cattle Raisers Association. He died in 1919.

Major K.M. Van Zandt, Marker Location: Northeast corner of Main and Exchange Ave. — Considered one of Fort Worth's founding fathers, Khleber Miller Van Zandt arrived in Fort Worth in 1865 and became part of just about every move to advance the fortunes of the city. He was by profession a lawyer. During the Civil War Van Zandt as a captain organized a company in the Seventh Texas Infantry. He fought in Mississippi and Tennessee before being taken as a prisoner by Union troops. After the war he was mustered out as a major and moved to Fort Worth to take part in several business ventures. In 1875 he rallied local citizens to take part in several business ventures. In 1875 he rallied local citizens to form a company to bring in the city's first railroad, which had made it only to Dallas. He helped start what was to become Fort Worth's leading bank, was co-founder of a newspaper and helped build the first streetcar system.

Bob Wills, Marker Location: In front of Billy Bob's Texas — Much of the music of Bob Wills came from the cotton fields of Texas, where he learned the musical styles of jazz and of the blues. Wills adopted the new music to his own and "Texas swing" was born. Wills moved to Fort Worth in 1929 to organize the now-classic sound of the Light Crust Doughboys. The group later was known as the Texas Playboys. In 1940 Wills recorded *New San Antonio Rose* and achieved national attention. He was featured in 19 movies. Although Wills never considered his music as country, he was elected to the Country Music Hall of Fame in 1968.

c h a p t e r

22 As the Millennium Ends

What's in store for the next 1,000 years?

That history is yet to be recorded.

What we do know is that Fort Worth ends the current millennium with a bang.

The Fort Worth Stock Show, which began in the Fort Worth Stockyards in 1896, was as popular as ever as it marked its centennial year in 1996.

Amid much deserved fanfare, the city in 1998 flocked to see the $65 million **Bass Performance Hall** in Sundance Square downtown. Spearhead Ed Bass and others visited performance halls over the world in deciding on the design of the 2,056-seat Bass Hall, which was built to last 300 years.

The last year of the century — and of the millennium — saw Texas Longhorns on the trail again as the City of Fort Worth celebrated its sesquicentennial — marking 150 years since pony soldiers rode here in 1849 to build a crude fort on the bluff overlooking the forks of the Trinity River.

To mark the sesquicentennial milestone, a permanent **Fort Worth Longhorn Herd** tended by seven drovers made itself at home in the Fort Worth Stockyards in 1999. The herd was to officially arrive with the **Chisholm Trail Roundup** parade June 12. The parade would be a short-term rebirth of two miles of the real Chisholm Trail.

Stockyards visitors later would marvel at real Texas Longhorns and see an authentic trail drive each day as the animals trailed from the Stockyards to graze on good grass along the nearby Trinity River.

Annual Events in the Stockyards

February — Cowtown Marathon and 10K Run starts and ends at Stockyards

February 8 — Re-enactment of shoot-out between Luke Short and "Longhair" Jim Courtwright at White Elephant Saloon.

March — Cowtown Goes Green. Parade and street party on St. Patrick's Day.

April — Weekly rodeos and Pawnee Bill Wild West Shows begin in Cowtown Coliseum, through mid-September.

June — Three-day Chisholm Trail roundup celebration throughout Stockyards.

September — Three-day Pioneer Days celebration throughout Stockyards.

October — Red Stegall Cowboy Gathering.

December — Buses leave Stockyards on Christmas tour of lights.

Maps

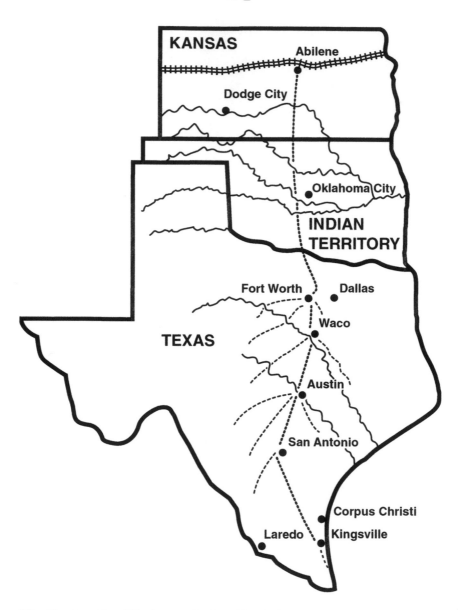

The Route - Fort Worth was the last bit of civilization as cowboys in the 1860's and 1870's trailed longhorns north on the Chisholm Trail to the railroad at Abilene, Kansas.

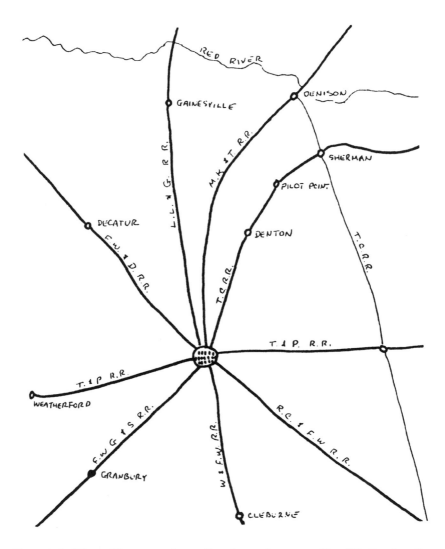

Tarantula Map - There wasn't a railroad anywhere near Fort Worth when the *Democrat* ran this map July 26, 1873 "showing the different Rail Roads centering at Fort Worth." One reader commented the map looked like a Tarantula. The map later proved prophetic as Fort Worth became a railroad center.

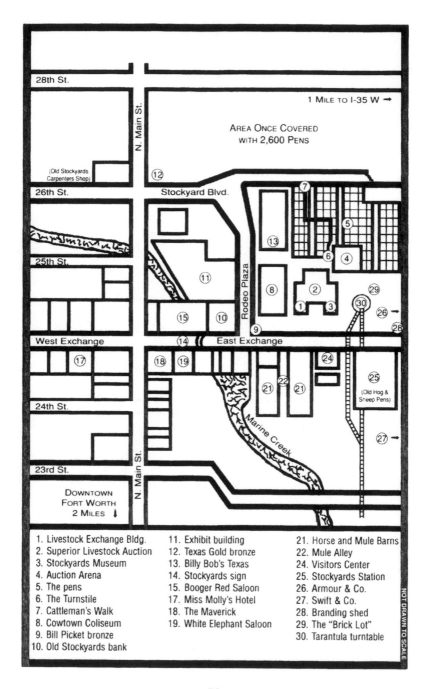

28th St.

N. Main St.

1 Mile to I-35 W →

Area Once Covered
with 2,600 Pens

(Old Stockyards
Carpenters Shop)

26th St.

Stockyard Blvd.

25th St.

Rodeo Plaza

West Exchange

East Exchange

24th St.

N. Main St.

23rd St.

Downtown
Fort Worth
2 Miles ↓

Marine Creek

(Old Hog &
Sheep Pens)

NOT DRAWN TO SCALE

1. Livestock Exchange Bldg.	11. Exhibit building	21. Horse and Mule Barns
2. Superior Livestock Auction	12. Texas Gold bronze	22. Mule Alley
3. Stockyards Museum	13. Billy Bob's Texas	24. Visitors Center
4. Auction Arena	14. Stockyards sign	25. Stockyards Station
5. The pens	15. Booger Red Saloon	26. Armour & Co.
6. The Turnstile	17. Miss Molly's Hotel	27. Swift & Co.
7. Cattleman's Walk	18. The Maverick	28. Branding shed
8. Cowtown Coliseum	19. White Elephant Saloon	29. The "Brick Lot"
9. Bill Picket bronze		30. Tarantula turntable
10. Old Stockyards bank		

Sources

Brice, Donaly E. *The Great Comanche Raid*. Austin: Askin Press, 1987.

Capps, Benjamin. *The Warren Wagon Train Raid*. Dallas: Southern Methodist University Press, 1989.

Garrett, Julia Kathryn. *Fort Worth: A Frontier Triumph*. Austin: The Encino Press, 1972.

Garrett, Kathryn and Lake, and Mary Daggett. *Down Historic Trails of Fort Worth and Tarrant County*. Fort Worth: Hodgkins, Co., 1949.

Goodwyn, Frank. *Life on the King Ranch*. College Station: Texas A&M University Press, 1951.

Hunter, J. Marvin, ed. *The Trail Drivers of Texas*. Austin: University of Texas Press, 1985.

Jaques, Mary J. *Texas Ranch Life*. College Station: Texas A&M University Press, 1989.

Johnson, Cecil. *Guts: Legendary Black Rodeo Cowboy Bill Pickett*. Fort Worth: The Summit Group, 1994.

Knight, Oliver. *Fort Worth: Outpost on the Trinity*. Norman: University of Oklahoma Press, 1953.

Lanning, Jim & Judy. *Texas Cowboys*. College Station: Texas A&M University Press, 1984.

Lauderdale, R.J. *Life on the Range and on the Trail*. San Antonio: The Naylor Company, 1936.

Paddock, B.B. *Early Days in Fort Worth, Much of Which I Saw and Part of Which I Was*. N.P., N.D. (At Fort Worth Public Library, local history room.)

Paddock, B.B. *History of Fort Worth, and the Northwest Edition.* Volumes 1-4. Chicago & New York: Lewis Publishing Co., 1922.

Pate, J'Nell L. *Livestock Legacy. The Fort Worth Stockyards.* College Station: Texas A&M University Press, 1988.

Pate, J'Nell L. *North of the River.* Fort Worth: Texas Christian University Press, 1994.

Sanders, Leonard. *How Fort Worth Became the Texasmost City.* Fort Worth: Texas Christian University Press, 1986.

Selcer, Richard F. *Hell's Half Acre.* Fort Worth: Texas Christian University Press, 1991.

Williams, Mack, ed. *The News-Tribune in Old Fort Worth, A Bicentennial Memory Book.* Fort Worth: Mack and Madeline Williams, 1975.